Surviving
ALASKA

Surviving ALASKA

This book may save your life.

---

by Mary Ames

foreword by Tim Mowry   illustrated by Bob Parsons

ALASKA BOOK
ADVENTURES™
Epicenter Press

Epicenter Press Inc.
Alaska Book Adventures™

Epicenter Press publishes books about art, history, nature, and diverse cultures and lifestyles of Alaska and the Pacific Northwest.

Epicenter Press
6524 NE 181st St. Suite 2
Kenmore, WA 98028.
www.Epicenterpress.com
www.Coffeetownpress.com
www.Camelpress.com

For more information go to: www.Epicenterpress.com

Library of Congress Control Number: 2008930291
ISBN: 9780979047008

"FEAR IS AN EMOTION
INDESPENSIBLE FOR SURVIVAL"

—HANNA ARENDT, GERMAN PHILOSOPHER

Foreword

In the more than two decades I've lived in Alaska, I've never had a life-threatening experience, unless you count all the times I should have died.

There was the time many years ago, before I came to appreciate the killer that Alaska can be, that my future wife, a friend, and I went canoeing in Paxson Lake—a large, deep, cold lake. We had a dog in the canoe. None of us wore life jackets, or knew squat about canoeing. Had we tipped over out in the middle of the lake, which we almost did, the dog would have had the best chance of surviving.

Then there was the time another friend and I decided to hike around the twenty-seven-mile Chena Dome Trail east of Fairbanks. I convinced my friend we could hike the trail in a single day, even though I had no clue what we were getting into.

We were unprepared. The trail was brutally hard. We had no camping, rain, or cold-weather gear. The only food we took was a few pieces of leftover chicken curry pizza and a couple of candy bars. We each had a quart of water—not enough.

It took us twenty hours of non-stop hiking to complete the hike, but we made it, thanks in large part to the fact the weather cooperated. Most of the hike was well above tree line. Had a storm come up, we would have been in trouble.

As it turned out, the most dangerous part of the hike was the drive home. We were so exhausted we could hardly stay awake.

Back in the days when I ran the Iditarod and Yukon Quest sled dog races, it was not uncommon to mush in temperatures of thirty or forty below. The coldest temperature I ever recall during a race was sixty-two degrees below zero on the Fortymile River. This was no big deal. We were prepared for it. We had the proper clothing and gear, which is one reason why no musher ever has died in either the Iditarod or Yukon Quest.

In Alaska, it's all about being prepared. And even then, that's no guarantee.

You never know when you might come around a bend in a trail or river and find yourself face to face with a grizzly bear. You never know when a moose might walk in front of your car.

Flip a canoe in a lake or river in Alaska and it's different than flipping a canoe in a lake or river in Illinois. The water is so cold in Alaska that it takes your breath away, even on a sizzling hot day when the sun stays out all night.

Forty below plays no favorites. Hypothermia is a household word in Alaska, whether you live in Juneau, Fairbanks, or Barrow. Cold kills people every year. All it takes is one little mistake or an unexpected turn of events, and you find yourself in a life or death situation.

I'll never forget the story I wrote for the *Fairbanks Daily News-Miner* about the two trappers who got stranded in the high country north of Fairbanks when their snowmachines got stuck in the bottom of a valley. They had no matches, so they soaked a stick with gas from one of the machines and then used the spark from their spark plug to get a fire started. They were rescued the next day—warm and dry—and returned a week later to retrieve their snowmachines.

It was so Alaskan that you had to love it.

Neither will I forget the comment from a Bush trapper who got lost in a storm on his snowmachine and ran out of gas. He was stranded for several days before searchers found him. He survived by fabricating a pot out of his empty gasoline can to melt snow for drinking water. It didn't taste great, but he lived to tell the story.

"I McGyver'ed my way out," he told a *News-Miner* reporter from his hospital bed, referring to the 1980s TV series about a secret agent who routinely escaped do-or-die crises with only a Swiss Army knife and Duct® tape.

In Alaska, sometimes what it takes to stay alive is simple common sense. The ability to improvise and adapt, if you have to—and you probably will—goes a long way in survival situations. Little things, like knowing how and having the makings to start a fire, can save your life.

Tim Mowry, outdoor editor
Fairbanks Daily News-Miner

Preface

Be suspicious of any book that purports to describe all of Alaska in one lump-no matter what the subject is. Alaska is big and diverse, comprised of vastly different climates and terrains.

Dressing correctly for a winter day in Southeast Alaska could invite serious frostbite in many other parts of the state. Likewise, dressing to survive a December day in Interior Alaska would have you over-dressed and overheated along the coast.

I discovered in my research that multitudes of books have been written directing people how to survive. Survival is a popular idea that existed long before the invention of the printing press.

Like history books, survival books are written by the "winners," so to speak. The authors may not have had their own harrowing experiences to prove their mettle, but they did survive, and that's what this book is all about. Why do some people die in the wilderness?

Often we can only speculate. Some mistakes will be made again and again.

What it comes down to, for me, is convincing people that things may not go as planned and that they should have a backup plan. In addition to planning ahead and anticipating trouble, survival has to do with thinking on your feet and being determined to get through the crisis of the moment with all body parts intact.

I hope this book will inform, entertain, stimulate some thought, and help readers skirt their own disasters.

Introduction

Alaska holds many opportunities for disaster. And you don't have to be far from the city to find yourself in trouble. A man was stomped to death by a moose on the University of Alaska Anchorage campus, and a grandmother was killed by a grizzly bear on a popular jogging trail on the outskirts of the city. In Fairbanks, a teenager lost her toes to frostbite after being locked out of her house unexpectedly.

Alaska has it all. Earthquakes, volcanoes, deep cold, tsunamis, avalanches, floods, and wildfires occur with regularity. Angry moose, defensive bears, killer mud flats, sinking boats, and aircraft that fall out of the sky all are part of life in this wonderful state. In the winter, it often gets cold enough in the northern half of the state to turn propane and fuel oil into gel.

An integral part of human nature believes, "It will never happen to me." Every year, skilled pilots crash, savvy fishermen lose boats, experienced hikers fall, cautious drivers slam into moose, and from one end of the state to the other life takes a sudden turn from joy to disaster.

The longer you are in Alaska, the greater the odds that you will find yourself in trouble some day. The information in this book can make a difference. Will you become the subject of an obituary in the newspaper, or will you come back from the brink with your own story about how you survived?

Eagles may regard your
small pets as a snack.

Table of Contents

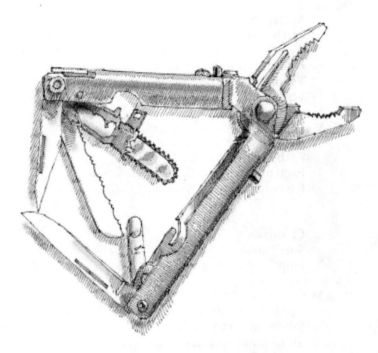

The more gear you carry that
serves multiple uses, the better.

Before You Go

So, let's get started. First, a question: What's in your pocket?

You might have all the sensible food and gear imaginable in your car, boat, or plane. But if the car goes over an embankment, the boat sinks, or the plane burns, what you have in your pockets may have to get you through a few grim hours or possibly days.

It is a good idea to have a waterproof container inside a pocket of whatever you're wearing. At the very least, you should have matches or butane lighter in that container and an all-purpose tool such as a Leatherman® or Swiss Army Knife and a whistle.

The more gear you can carry that serves multiple functions, the better your chances of one day being able to tell your story—"...and there I was, with just a (fill in the blank) for survival."

Wrap your survival gear in a space blanket. It can help you stay warm. Spread out on the ground, its reflection can be a signal to search and rescue folks who are looking for you.

A parachute cord has many uses. You might not be stranded long enough to discover all of them. Fifty feet of cord will not take up much room. You can use it to make snares or to lash branches into a secure shelter. You can fashion a fish trap from it, also.

Large garbage bags can be used to make rain ponchos, fish nets, and water basins.

A reliable, lightweight flashlight is nice to have. But candles provide light and heat, and the melted wax can be used to get a wood fire burning hotter and brighter.

Don't forget safety pins, a small but invaluable item. They can be useful in all the customary ways—fastening clothes, picking out splinters, replacing screws in eyeglasses—and in some unusual ways too, such as fashioning hooks to catch fish.

Mosquito repellent that has one hundred percent Deet® literally can save your life in the summer, and makes a good fire starter, too.

You are limited only in space, money, and imagination when you assemble your survival gear. The bigger and bulkier your package is, the higher odds you will not have it with you when you need it most.

And before you head out, even for a short jaunt, tell a responsible adult where you are going, how you are going to get there, and when you plan to return.

PLANNING AHEAD

Human nature is the same in Alaska as elsewhere. We think bad things will never happen to us because there are so many people in line ahead of us. But all the advice about planning for a disaster, be it high winds or high water, remains the same.

- Have a radio that runs on batteries or can be handcranked for power.

- Have a flashlight or headlamp and candles.

- Make sure your smoke detectors are working.

- Have plenty of extra batteries for everything that will need them, including batteries for your hearing aid.

- Have a cell phone or a satellite phone with you, preferably with a crank charger.

- Have at least three gallons of drinking water per person stored in your home in food-safe containers. Change the water every three months. If you need to disinfect the water, add two drops of unscented household bleach per gallon.

- Have on hand extra supplies of special needs such as prescription medicine.

- Keep your car's gas tank at least half-full at all times, to be prepared for a fast, long getaway should you need to make one.

- Attach the proper wrenches and written shut-off instructions for propane tanks, hot-water heaters, and fuel tanks.

- Have an emergency plan for your family in the event you are separated during an emergency.

- Have an evacuation plan for your family.

- After a disaster strikes, don't return to your home until you are certain it is safe.

- Give yourself some time to clear your head before you make big decisions.

- Make an inventory of what you have and move forward.

Stay alert and use caution
in the backcountry.

Critters (Large)

BEARS

A big draw in Alaska are the wild critters that roam the backcountry and are seen regularly sauntering through urban areas. You see bears in Juneau, the state capital, and moose regularly wander nonchalantly through Anchorage and Fairbanks. Barrow and other coastal villages in the north and west get the occasional polar bear searching for good eats around town.

Though it may seem obvious, it needs to be said that as wonderful as it is to see wild animals, they are not pets. They are furry, but don't want to be cuddled by humans. Usually you don't know what experiences an animal has had before you encounter it, so you don't know its mood.

While many people are thrilled to view wild animals, they want a single, sure-fire way to stay safe when an animal shows its wild side. Wild animals, unrefined by culture and civilization, don't read books. They don't know how to act predictably. The only sure way to be safe is to stay away from them, if you can. This may not be possible, so stay alert and use caution when you step off the pavement.

Do as I say, not as I do

There are enough scary bear stories to fill books, and, in fact, they do fill books—scores of them. There are enough bear tales to give the jitters to everyone around the campfire.

Years ago, I was introduced to the joys of bear-watching. It was blueberry season, and while my camping companion was out picking berries, he spotted a black bear sow and a cub. When he returned quietly to our tent, he whispered about the bears and insisted I take a look.

I thought he was crazy. Sneaking up on a sow and cub is something you don't do. And we'd already had a bear visitor. We'd both been out picking berries, and hadn't gone far or been gone long. When we returned, the old olive-drab tent was torn where a bear had walked through it. There was little other damage, but it spooked me that something so big could be so close, quick, and quiet.

At any rate, we found the sow and cub that day, and watched them for a while. We were not seen and the bears didn't smell us, as we were downwind. I've enjoyed every bear I've been fortunate enough to see in the wild—numerous blackies and a few grizzlies.

Bears are quick and quiet. They have proven deadly when people were acting like idiots, and they have killed people who did everything right in bear country and showed respect for them.

Alaska bears come in three flavors—white, black, and brown. They occupy their own geographic areas and different places on the food chain. You could be on the menu if a bear is not a picky eater. All bears have a great sense of smell, strong curiosity abetted by sharp claws and teeth, the ability to run up to thirty-six miles per hour and, well—the strength of a bear.

BLACK BEARS

Black bears adapt well to human populations, which means they don't mind hanging out in the suburbs. Although the smallest of the three species, black bears can grow to a weight of several hundred pounds and can do lots of damage simply to satisfy their persistent curiosity. They can climb trees. They are most likely to be found in grassy meadows when the snow melts, around berry patches, near salmon streams in the fall, and anywhere that garbage accumulates if they haven't retreated to their den in winter. In spite of their name, their colors range from light cinnamon, to blue, and of course black. Except for a sow and her cubs, black bears usually don't hang out in groups.

BROWN BEARS

Brown bears, which in the Interior also are called grizzlies, are larger than black bears with prominent shoulder humps and long noses. They do not acclimate to human populations as well as black bears. However, in the spring of their second year, when momma chases them away, the wandering adolescents bumble around looking for their place in the world. With luck on everyone's part, their visit to urban areas will be a brief respite before they disappear into the hinterlands. They use their claws for digging up marmots and below-ground mammals. These bears like open areas, love berry patches, and congregate near salmon streams during spawning runs.

A standard Alaska joke: When you climb a tree to escape a bear and it follows you up the tree, it is a black bear. If it knocks the tree over to get you, it is a brown bear.

POLAR BEARS

The great white bears of the far north subsist primarily on seals and other bounty from the sea. In "normal" years, they are land-locked on the coast shores during summer and found out on pack ice in the winter. But their usual patterns appear to have been disrupted by Arctic warming that may be altering their habitat and keeping them on land for longer periods.

The standard advice for traveling and camping in bear country is to be keenly aware of your surroundings at all times, though beyond this advice there is some disagreement. The conventional advice is to be noisy when hiking so you don't inadvertently sneak up on a bear, though some believe that making noise—especially in areas where bears have been accustomed to the presence of humans—will actually *attract* bears, especially those who remember snacking on human food leftovers. When you see a bear, give it distance and plenty of room to escape without coming near you. Keep in mind that your chances of avoiding detection by a bear will be much improved if you are downwind from it. A bear smells a lot better than it sees.

According to conventional wisdom, if a bear comes after you, the best defense is to play dead if your attacker is a grizzly bear, but fight like hell if it is a black bear. Running away from any bear is always considered to be a bad idea. Many experts believe it is better to back away, slowly, if you can. Other experts, however, believe humans can retain some control in a confrontation by *moving* away slowly, not *backing* away. This difference is pretty subtle. There is no one single guaranteed way to survive these close encounters. The main thing is to put some distance between you and the bear as best you can.

Take measures to avoid attracting bears. Keep your surroundings clean, with both food and garbage secured either out of the bear's reach or in bear-proof containers. This includes bird feed and pet food. Do not cover your food containers with pepper spray because this may attract rather than repel a bear. Cook and store food downwind from the campsite, with good visibility in all directions.

Bears are attracted by petroleum products, or items that contain petroleum products. Marine and aviation fuel should be secured out of reach.

If you understand the basics of firearm safety and shoot well enough to hit a target on a regular basis, you should consider carrying a firearm for protection. In my opinion, the best defensive weapon is a shotgun, which can be packed around easily. Others believe a large-caliber weapon is best for self-defense. For everyone's sake, however, if you are not familiar with guns, you shouldn't rely on one. Keep in mind, too, that if you are traveling in a national park, of which there are many in Alaska, you are forbidden from carrying firearms for protection.

The park service policy on firearms possession would be loosened if the National Rifle Association and its allies in Congress get their way. Currently, the regulation says that "unloaded weapons may be possessed within a temporary lodging or mechanical mode of conveyance when such implements are rendered temporarily inoperable, or are packed, cased, or stored in a manner that will prevent their ready use."

So, we take that to mean you can carry a firearm legally if you are in camp or at a cabin, or are moving around in a boat, all-terrain vehicle, or airplane, but your firearms would not be much use for defense if you are attached by a bear while hiking.

The other option in case of a direct assault is pepper spray. This appears to work most but not all the time. Some people recommend trying to make yourself seem larger by spreading your arms wide. Some people suggest yelling forcefully.

For many years, the conventional wisdom has been that wearing bells on clothes and packs and making noise, especially in areas with high brush and limited visibility, will let bears know you are coming and they will head in the other direction. But many believe this advice has worn out its usefulness, that the tinkling of bells may stimulate a bear's curiosity and attract some bears that associate the human noise with a potential source of camp scraps carelessly left behind. Your best bet is to seek local advice. What bear defenses may be appropriate when you're camping in a wilderness area far from most human activity may not be the same near a busy recreational area on the Kenai Peninsula.

Keep in mind that your actions around bears can have long-term effects on them. If you help them to become accustomed to humans and human food, you may be signing their death warrants. An acclimated bear is dangerous and will become a problem for someone in the future.

A cautionary tale about dogs and moose

The late Susan Butcher, four-time winner of the Iditarod Trail Sled Dog Race, was favored to win the race to Nome in 1985 when her team was knocked out of the race after being attacked by a moose. Several dogs were injured seriously.

In *Iditarod Classics* by Lew Freedman, a book of first-person stories about exciting moments in the race, musher Dewey Halverson describes being the first musher to arrive on the scene.

"The dogs were trying to make themselves disappear into the snow. It was dead quiet and there's this big cow moose standing right in the middle of the team. I walked up and shot her twice. The moose had her head down. I must have hit her because she turned around and started up the trail, went up to the front of the team and started kicking more dogs. Then you could hear dogs screaming.

"I was waiting to get another shot. There were a couple of trees along the trail. Pretty soon she turned around, put her head down, and started coming right to the sled after us. I knew it was warfare by that time. I had three more bullets and no extras, so I shot two more times and, finally, on the third shot, she stopped. She just stood there and all of a sudden I could see her wobble. Then over she went. BOOM!"

If you are forced to kill a bear in defense of life or property, you must notify the state Department of Fish & Game. You must surrender the skull and hide. This means you must noy only skin out the bear, but haul out the hide, which will be heavy, wet, gritty, and smell awful.

MOOSE

Moose kill people, too, but usually not without provocation. The problem is that you may not be the provoker but are just in the wrong place at the wrong time. When a moose goes on a rampage, look out!

In an incident at the University of Alaska Anchorage, a moose quietly browsed some trees on campus, minding its own business, when some students began pelting the big animal with snowballs. The

moose was confined on one side of a building and apparently felt cornered. Instead of going after the students, the moose attacked and killed a seventy-year-old man who happened to be in its escape path.

Know this: an angry or threatened moose will have its ears laid back and the fur on its neck will bristle. If you see this, run away as fast as you can—no need to be subtle.

Mother moose are protective of their young. Bull moose in rut can be dangerous. Stay away. Deep snows with no easy path of escape can motivate a moose to fight rather than give ground. Give all moose some respectable distance and an escape route.

Moose are hazards along Alaska's roads and highways, too. They are big, around fifteen hundred pounds. Even calves born in the spring weigh several hundred pounds by fall. If you hit a moose with your car while traveling at a high speed, chances are you and your passengers will be injured and the moose will be dead.

BE ALERT

In the fall, moose do a lot of grazing and they are seen more often on the grassy edges of the road. Before the snows come, the fall season is dark and the moose become almost invisible at night and you might not seen them until the last few seconds as you arrive around a bend in the road doing sixty miles per hour. It pays to be alert. One telltale mark is the crescent of lighter fur that runs along the sides of their bellies. That slim sliver of silver might be your distant early warning.

Keep your eyes on the broad picture while driving, not just straight down the road. Passengers should be watchful, too. Moose can come at you from either side of the road, unexpectedly, at any time. This is especially true where brush has grown up alongside the road.

If you are cruising down the highway, see a moose crossing directly in front of you, and realize in an instant that you will not be able to stop in time, take evasive action. It might be wiser to veer into a snowbank than hit a moose. Count yourself lucky if you have such a soft landing site handy. The argument for evasive action is this: The typical moose, in addition to weighing the better part of a ton, also stands six to eight feet tall on long, spindly legs. In a typical collision, the car strikes the legs first, upending the moose and the huge animal typically falls sideways directly onto the windshield. Ouch!

IF YOU HAVE AN ACCIDENT

You must notify the Alaska State Troopers, or local police, right away if you crash into a moose, or vice versa.

Approach the downed animal cautiously. A still and seemingly dead moose can come back to life swiftly. Watch for any sign of breathing. Use a tree limb or piece of brush to check for reactions. A dead animal's eyes will be open and the unlucky creature will show no reaction when touched.

If you are one of those Alaskans who tend to a lawn in the summer, remember that a pile of grass clippings will attract moose in the fall just as a garden will attract the big animals during the summer. Put your grass clippings where these big, lumbering animals can't do damage. For example, you might be sorry if you leave your clippings next to an elevated outdoor fuel tank. Keep in mind, too, moose will stomp your dog if the mood strikes.

Again, the best all-around advice is this: Give the moose plenty of room to maneuver.

WILD CANINES

Common wisdom says that a healthy wolf never attacks a human. One of my friends always replies to that remark by saying the absence of living victims doesn't prove anything. She maintains wolves always did attack, but never left traces of their human victims.

Your pets are a different matter. They definitely are prey, as residents of outlying neighborhoods around Fairbanks and Anchorage have learned in recent years. If you keep your dogs chained in the yard, or next to an unattended campsite, you could find shredded fur where your dogs used to be. It doesn't happen too often, but it does happen.

The large population of wolves has increased the spread of diseases such as mange. The disease, first noticed on the Kenai Peninsula, has migrated north of the Alaska Range. Sick animals are stressed animals, which makes them unpredictable.

Fox are abundant too. Red and cross fox roam south of the Brooks Range while the arctic fox inhabits the northern areas. They are most often seen in open fields hunting rodents. Foxes, especially the arctic fox, are susceptible to rabies. They c infect a dog yard. A rabid anim can appear tame and approach humans. Someone who learned everything they know about animal behavior from Walt Disney movies might interpret this

curiosity as an act of friendship. Don't believe it!

A rabid animal must be shot and the body handled only while wearing protective gear.

EAGLES

Eagles will regard your small pets much as wolves do—a snack. An eagle reportedly snatched a little yapper in close proximity to humans just outside of a motor home in Valdez in 1993.

Urban legend or fact? The only way to make sure your pets are safe is to keep them in the house, in an enclosed kennel, or on a leash at all times. This works out well because these are also ways to prevent your pet from harassing the wildlife.

Wolves interrupt ski trip

Most people who have lived in Alaska their entire lives have never seen a wolf, let alone a pack of them. And most packs of wolves are seen from the air, not from the ground in the middle of nowhere.

Alan Kendall, a middle-school teacher, had the experience of a lifetime while cross-country skiing solo on the frozen Tanana River from Nenana to Fairbanks. It was a beautiful, sunny Saturday morning in early April.

Kendall rounded a bend in the river and noticed several stray dogs ahead. They seemed out of place because the nearest house was miles away. Then, suddenly, the number of "dogs" increased to ten.

It was a pack of wolves!

The gray, black, and brown wolves were playing with one another and at first did not see, hear, or smell Kendall, who was upwind on the big river. "They were huge," Kendall said.

"During that thirty seconds I looked for an escape route," Kendall told reporter Tim Mowry of the *Fairbanks Daily News-Miner.*

"I couldn't go left or right to either riverbank; the snow was too crusty or deep, and the banks were too far away." Kendall considered turning around, but "I didn't dare turn my back to them."

Kendall said he felt like a "pork chop." After contemplating the situation briefly, he figured his best option was to move forward. "I charged toward them, skiing as fast as I could, yelling at the top of my lungs," he said, "Every two or three pole strokes, I'd yell."

Two of the wolves peeled off to the left, and three moved off to the right, disappearing into the woods. But the remaining five at first remained about fifty yards ahead of the skier, and then one by one circled around behind him. Finally, they lost interest and moved on.

Kendall, a former helicopter pilot, had seen plenty of wolves from the air but nothing compared to his experience that brilliantly sunny day in April. "I'm glad it happened, and I'm glad it's behind me," he told the *News-Miner.*

Do not underestimate
the dreaded mosquitoes!

Bugs That Bite

The good news is the lack of poisonous insects in Alaska, at least not yet. Global warming may change that. Still, it's a tough life for bugs in places where temperatures can remain below freezing, even well-below zero, for weeks on end.

According to old sourdough tales, the best bed at roadhouses and bunk houses was the one next to an uninsulated outside wall because the cold kept the bed bugs away.

Flying insects that bite, like most bugs in the north, have a limited season. For most of the year, they are out of commission, but when their time is here, the swarms are impressive. I usually prefer to enter my Zen space when the bugs are biting a bit and wearing protective clothes when they get thicker and meaner. Only when they are unbearable do I reach for the repellent, but when I need it, nothing else will do.

Hot, dry summers bring out wasps, specifically yellow jackets, in abundance. Wasps bite and sting. If you want to get rid of them, you can wait until the weather cools, or make a trap with meat or juice as bait.

MOSQUITOES

Many people venture into the hinterlands and never face a threat from four-legged beasts. But you can count on becoming a meal for biting insects if you spend time in the woods, on the tundra, or even on the outskirts of most towns in the warm months. In Southeast, the mosquitoes are less common. But in the Interior and Arctic, they are plentiful, hungry, and relentless.

In the arctic and subarctic, swarms of mosquitoes can become so thick that you can't breathe without netting. They may be small, but in groups they can kill humans and large animals with their voracious blood sucking. Do not underestimate them! Mosquitoes like warm weather, but not bright, hot sun. A good wind will get rid of them, too.

SAND FLIES & BLACK FLIES

When the mosquitoes have thinned out late in the summer after their second hatching, you'll start to see the "white-socks," also known as sand flies or black files. These nasty little critters will take a hunk out of your skin, leave a welt bigger than a mosquito bite, and may fly full speed into your eyes, ears, or nose.

NO-SEE-UMS

These dreaded little critters are much easier to see once they have gorged on your blood, but they still very tiny. They don't make noise, but they have a fierce bite, surprisingly so for their size. Unless your screens are sized down for no-see-ums, you might become a midnight snack. Their bites are big and itch mightily.

Some people use insect repellent, others do not. That is your decision. But it is a good precaution to have repellent with you all summer because you also can use it for fire starter and paint remover. It is powerful stuff, but it will wear off. Sweat also washes it off, so you will need to replenish frequently on a long, strenuous hike and in other situations in which you get wet.

Even if you use repellent and it works for you most of the time, a few insects won't get the message that they are supposed to be repelled. Switching brands might help repel some bugs that liked to use your previous brand as a cocktail.

Other defensive measures including wearing light-colored, loose-fitting clothes that can be tied, taped, or buttoned closed at the wrists, neck, and ankles. Wear heavy fleece or leather gloves that the blood-suckers can't bite through. Wear a head net. Smoke a cigar. Sit next to a smoky

No West Nile Virus has been seen,
but surveillance continues.

campfire. A coil of PIC® repellent smoldering around camp helps keep the bugs down, too.

As of early 2008, the West Nile Virus had not arrived in Alaska aboard birds or mosquitoes. One man died from the virus, but he apparently contracted the disease Outside. At last report, scientists were debating whether the virus would migrate as far north as Alaska.

"If you find a dead bird of the [suspect] species and or a group of dead birds of any species, do not pick up the bird," the federal agency warns.

Meanwhile, surveillance continues. In Alaska, the most likely bird species to contract the virus are ravens, crows, magpies, several species of jays, eagles, falcons, hawks, and owls. The U.S. Fish and Wildlife Service requests that birds suspected to have been electrocuted, shot, poisoned, "or otherwise killed under suspicious circumstances" be reported to its law enforcement division at 800-858-7621, or 907-271-2828 in Anchorage.

Bureaucrats can be a nuisance,
but are rarely life-threatening.

Critters (The Human Kind)

The state attracts many people who find the Lower 48 too confining, want to get away from something or someone (fill in the blank: a corporate career, spouse, parents, parole officer, etc.), or who just can't get along elsewhere.

Many artists, actors, and other creative people love the freedom they find in the expansive northern state. Alaska also attracts the occasional refugee from the dark side, including people with mental illness and/or criminal backgrounds. We call these refugees end-of-the-roaders because often they settle in villages at the end of a road somewhere on Alaska's thin highway system. Many roads end in the wilderness. Most of the time this works out OK, but every few years you'll read in the newspaper reports about end-of-the-roaders damaging property, assaulting neighbors, and even murdering innocent people.

The lesson here is to mind your own business and give the locals the space they need.

Respect private property—relative to the size of Alaska, there's not much of it. Honor those "no trespassing" signs. Assume everyone you meet is armed.

Don't come between an Alaskan and ice cream, alcohol, or a chance to go fishing.

If you come to visit Alaska with the idea of dropping in to surprise an old friend, or a friend of a friend, be prepared to hear, "I don't have any friends." Summer can mean an endless stream of visitors who didn't move to the state for social opportunities.

Some basic rules that may help you get a sincere invitation to return:

Remember the fish rule. Fish and guests begin to stink after three days.

Chip in for food, booze, and travel expenses. Alaskans detest freeloaders. This is especially true in a bar.

Bring a gift that shows you thought of your hosts before you needed a place to sleep, shower, and wash your clothes.

Lend a hand with whatever needs to be done.

Be prepared to entertain yourself while your hosts go off to earn a living.

Buying a round for the house. Most bars in Alaska have a bell hanging from the ceiling. Ring the bell if you want to buy a round for the house—this means everyone in the bar. If you don't have enough money to buy drinks, don't mess with the bell. This is no joke. Alaskans take this bar custom very seriously.

BUREAUCRATS
(THE REAL THREAT)

While you may or may not get a chance to see a four-legged furry critter in Alaska, there is a whole subspecies that thrives in such abundance that you can't avoid a sighting or two—the Bureaucrats. They can be a nuisance but are rarely life-threatening.

Alaskans, many of whom have libertarian tendencies, enjoy making fun of bureaucrats. It's a form of sport. Per capita, Alaska has more than twice the national average of these creatures—bureaucrats, that is, not libertarians, although the latter are in abundance, too. At any rate, one out of every three people in Alaska fits into the bureaucrat category. If they are not dressed in uniform with acronyms on the sleeve, you can identify them by attitudes and speech.

Listen for phrases such as "individual input" or "scoping session" or "not prudent" or "at this point in time." Their attitude is that they may allow you to do something on their land, which is most of Alaska.

Although they are more predictable than furry critters, some advice remains the same. Be aware of your surroundings. Leave them an out. Do not make threatening gestures.

Two famous proverbs:

"When in Rome, do as the Romans do." (When visiting a foreign land, such as Alaska, follow local customs.)

"We don't give a damn how they do it Outside." (The message is more or less the same, but with an Alaska attitude.)

A clue to the mentality of many Alaskans is found in the second proverb, which first appeared as a bumper sticker in Alaska with the influx of outsiders who came during construction of the trans-Alaska pipeline in the 1970s.

In addition, it is not a good idea to try to engage in normal conversation. Put a noncommittal half-smile on your face. Extend both arms in front of you at chest level with palms out. Back slowly away.

WILDFIRES

Wildfires are part and parcel of summer in Alaska, where hundreds of thousands of acres are blackened each year. Of course, humans are responsible for some of the fires, but many result from natural causes. Lightning, for example, has a propensity to strike the boreal forests, which consist of spruce, birch, aspen, and willow. Sensors have recorded more than 26,000 lightning strikes in a season.

Fires change the air quality from clear to hazy to no visibility at all, depending on the wind. Sometimes the gook in your lungs is from fires that are surprisingly far away.

If you are hiking or camping and see smoke and possibly flames heading in your direction, this is what you can do to minimize the danger:

- Head to lower ground; fires most often travel uphill.
- Find a place with a few trees, and wet ground, such as a river or creek.
- Travel perpendicular to the wind. Keep in mind that fire travels with the wind, but a big fire can create its own wind.
- Monitor a radio for reports on the fire.

If your home, recreation site, or campsite is in an area of fire activity, here are a few steps you can take to prepare for a rapid but orderly evacuation:

- Park your vehicle pointed in the direction of your retreat with the keys in the ignition.

Careless people start many fires

Wildfires aren't a problem throughout Alaska. Southeast's rain forests are too wet to burn, the Aleutian Chain, much of the west coast and the northern coastal areas don't have trees. Coastal areas, including Southcentral Alaska, usually don't have many lightning strikes.

Interior Alaska is where most of the summer fires flare, flame, and die a natural death.

However, people start fires, too, and the most dangerous time is after breakup (known as spring Outside) and before green up. This seems to be the time people do amazingly stupid things year after year in spite of repeated warnings.

When the dirt, dead leaves, and grass are tinder dry, Alaskans seem to love cleaning up by burning stuff in burn barrels, without screens, a water hose, or other safety precautions. Kids play with matches and fireworks in dead grass. People dump ashes that aren't completely cold and wet from stoves and burn barrels. Every year, several fires start from all of the above.

Sometimes the people get fined and have to pay damages. Sometimes not. We all get to see the scars for years afterward.

- Close doors and windows
- Store flammable materials such as paint and oily rags in sealed metal containers.
- Trees and shrubs should be cleared at least thirty feet from the house. Lawn and deck furniture should be moved away.
- Attach hoses to the outdoor spigots.

If you are traveling by car, stay tuned to the radio for announcement of road closures. Most wildfires are allowed to burn without suppression, the exceptions being fires in inhabited areas. But all fires are monitored. If you are flying:

- Check with flight service for restricted areas around fires.
- Be aware of increased air traffic around fires.
- Be prepared to make a change in your route of travel to avoid smoke. Plan ahead.
- Be aware the smoke can turn your skies dark enough suddenly to require flight instruments. Avoid being trapped.

The colder it is, the longer a car needs to be plugged in.

Driving

Most vehicles used north of the Alaska Range have a cord hanging out of the front end. The other end of the cord should be connected to an engine block heater, an oil pan heater, and/or possibly a battery blanket or heating pad. The purpose, of course, is to keep the innards of the vehicle warm enough to start when the temperature plummets.

Check the outlet to make sure it is on. You can use a lighted plug, also called an "idiot light" or some other appliance that indicates the presence of electricity. If built to code, outdoor outlets are supposed to be Ground Fault Interrupters, which in non-technical terms means they trip themselves off more easily than regular outlets. There are two tabs on the outlet labeled "test" and "reset." Press the reset. If the outlet still doesn't work, check the breaker box or fuse box. Flip the switch or replace the fuse if necessary.

The colder the temperature, the longer the vehicle needs to be plugged in. When it is thirty degrees below (Fahrenheit) or colder, consider leaving your car plugged in overnight. Remember that the longer the cord, the greater resistance, so park as close as you can to the outlet and use a short cord.

When the block heater is broken or your vehicles dies or has a flat tire out on the road, the electrical plug won't do you any good.

For a cold-soaked car, you may need an external heat source to warm the engine. The best option is a heater with no open flame. If your only source of heat has an open flame, do not put it directly under the vehicle. Use stove pipe ducting or some other means of directing warm air beneath the engine.

You should tent the vehicle if possible to keep the heat warming the engine and not the great outdoors. Tarps, old sleeping bags, or blankets can be draped over the hood to hold the heat where you need it.

Carpet scraps came in handy for one couple that used them to skirt the underside of their car when it wouldn't start in spite of being plugged in at sixty below.

GAS FILTER

FROZEN GAS LINE

Keeping your gas tank less than half full and parking it in a heated garage invites moisture to condense in the fuel tank and lines. Then, when you drive the car, and park out in the cold again, the moisture freezes, blocking the flow of fuel. This is a common Alaska problem. If your vehicle runs rough, or not at all, in the cold, a bottle of HEET® can help clear the lines. Many drivers add it each time they fill up in super cold weather as a preventative measure.

ICE ROADS AND BRIDGES

You just flew into Bethel and hailed a taxi. Should you protest when the driver takes you to the Kuskokwim River ice instead of the road? Not to worry, the river becomes the equivalent of a highway once the ice is solid. People drive on it with customary and traditional abandon.

In Fairbanks, the Chena River is used as a bridge between otherwise disconnected roads on the lower end near where the Chena flows into the Tanana River. These winter short cuts are customary ways of shaving a few miles off your trip.

At least once a year, especially around break-up, a vehicle goes through the ice somewhere in Alaska. A spell of warm weather in mid-winter can make the ice unsafe, too.

Some precautions to keep in mind:

- Islands and shoals make for thin ice. Give them wide berth.
- Ice will be thinnest at the edge of lakes and rivers.
- If you cross a lake that is fed by a river, make every effort to avoid the area where the current flows.
- Repeated crossings make the ice more fragile.
- Drive with your windows rolled down. If your car goes through the ice, abandon the vehicle through a window. Get to solid ice, flatten your body to spread out the weight, and wiggle to safety. If help is too far to get to on foot, build a fire, dry off, and wait for a rescue.
- If you go through the ice on the Chena River at Pike's Landing in Fairbanks, you will be within walking distance of three bars, where a couple of hot buttered rums will help transform an unpleasant episode into a funny story.

SAFE LODGING

Many lodges and hotels in Alaska are picturesque and historic, but old wooden buildings require special precautions to ensure a safe stay.

For starters, find out where the nearest emergency exit is, and make certain you can get through it. Check the exit door in winter to ensure that it is not frozen shut.

Find out where the nearest water source is. Not all rooms or even all floors have running water in old buildings.

If you are staying on an upper floor, have a good sturdy rope with you. You might need to rappel out the window in case of fire.

In old wooden lodges, locate the nearest emergency exit.

Give all sweepers a wide berth.
Tie all gear into the boat or canoe
so it is not easily swept away.

Floating

Alaska is blessed with vastly more river miles than roads. Rivers are used by people in riverboats, air boats, airplanes, snowmachines, and dog mushers. Rivers are roads except during breakup and freeze up.

Rivers close to towns and villages can get crowded with racers, adventure seekers, fishermen, hunters, and trappers. The Yukon River, accessible in several places by road, is popular with adventure seekers floating from Dawson City, Yukon, to Eagle or Circle City. People wanting to float the entire length are often foiled by Alaska's short summer season.

For a solitary float trip, you have to fly out to a more remote river. You won't have to watch out for other people, but the sweepers will still be there.

SWEEPERS

Sweepers are trees, roots, and logs that overhang riverbanks and lakes. Be very wary of them because they do, as the name suggests, sweep objects out of boats, canoes, and rafts and into the water. They also create whirlpools, and they can block the boat's forward travel while the current continues to push it from behind—a recipe for disaster. Give all sweepers a wide berth. Tie all gear into the boat or canoe so it is not easily swept away.

EXPERIENCE

REFLEXES

Find a pilot who has logged
at least a few thousand hours.

Flying

FINDING A GOOD PILOT

If you are going to get to the best places in Alaska, you have to go by air. You might find someone who offers to take you on a flight as a friend, take a scheduled flight on one of the many air services, or charter an air taxi service. Flying comes with an inherent risk. If your plane goes down, you might be hundreds of miles from help. But you can make your adventure safer by knowing what to expect and how to be a good passenger.

Talk to your pilot before you fly. Although the pilot is not required to answer, you can ask how many Alaska hours he or she has logged (you want to fly with someone who has a few thousand hours at least) and how often he has flown the route you are planning to take. The pilot has ultimate charge of the airplane and a good pilot wants passengers to be comfortable and happy.

If your charter flight is a seasonal job for someone who recently moved to Alaska, keep looking for a pilot. If you smell alcohol, forget it! If the pilot is erratic, boastful, or incoherent, the odds are working against you.

The Federal Aviation Administration (FAA) issues a little card that on one side lists the questions passengers have a right to ask and on the other lists passenger responsibilities. Some things are obvious such as the need for a seat and seat belt for every passenger, and instructions on how to get out of the airplane in an emergency. But you also need to know the location of the emergency locator transmitter (ELT) and how to set it off manually; the location of the fire extinguisher(s); what survival gear is on board, and where it is stowed. You also can expect the pilot to explain how the cargo is tied down. Ask about the weather along your route. Make certain the pilot has filed a flight plan. No pilot should be evasive or resent the questions.

Bring your earplugs and dress for survival in the event of an emergency landing. As extra insurance, give one of your reliable friends the who-what-when-where and time of return for your flight.

Pilots have the final say on loading the aircraft, so don't try to sneak extra gear on board and don't lie about your weight. Don't insist that the pilot make fewer trips with heavier loads to get your hunting or fishing party in and out quicker—and less expensively. Don't challenge a pilot to land if he is reluctant to do so. If there is an emergency, do exactly what the pilot tells you to do. Accept the pilot's go or no-go decisions regarding weather. No matter how much you want to be somewhere else, no matter that the clock is ticking away on your vacation or fishing trip, remember that it is bad form to whine about being alive on the ground.

Many passengers become nervous on the approach to a landing area and begin to act out their anxiety by starting to chat with the pilot. Try not to do this, especially if you're landing at an airport. The pilot needs to focus on the task at hand as well as communicate on the radio. Save the conversation for when you are on the ground.

UNDERSTANDING THE GAME

The route to the top is almost always the same for anyone who dreams of becoming a commercial pilot. Get your flight instructor rating and then build hours on someone else's time while teaching them to fly. Next step is air-taxi work, which consists of long hours, less pay when not flying, and waiting on the weather—all the while building hours. Not all air-taxi pilots are training for another job. Some of them love to fly in Alaska, have decades of experience in the state, and would never want to move on up to the big airlines. These are the pilots you want.

EMERGENCY LANDINGS

What if your pilot is suddenly incapacitated? A pilot and passenger returning from a successful hunt had just that experience. The last thing the pilot remembers is the back-seat passenger asking if he was all right. His next memory is of waking up in the intensive-care unit at the hospital. The happy ending—no injuries to the people, no damage to the airplane—was due in large part to the pilot setting up the landing well and the passenger keeping his wits about

him. What do you mean the pilot set up the landing well. This is unclear. Was the plane on final approach when the pilot passed out? Can you add more details?

A standard pilot joke is that you can land anywhere once. The procedures we discuss in this section are for emergencies in which you need to do exactly that—land once—with minimum damage to all concerned. If you are a frequent passenger, you should consider taking a short course on how to land a plane in an emergency.

If you find yourself at the controls of a plane you do not know how to fly, keep in mind that it is not necessary to land immediately, unless you are low on fuel. You will have either a stick or a yoke in your hands and rudders at your feet. The nose of the aircraft responds to the movement of the yoke/stick. If the stick is moved forward, the nose will go down. If the stick is pulled back, the nose will go up. Yoke to the right, the plane turns to the right; yoke to the left, the plane turns left. The rudders are used to make the turns coordinated, as in left stick, left rudder. The throttle is a knob on either the instrument panel or on the pilot's side of the plane, and it should be labeled. Forward throttle gives the engine more fuel and power; a backward throttle reduces power. To get used to the controls, practice keeping the plane straight and level at first, then do low-angle turns to the right and left, and then climb and descend.

Switch the radio frequency to the emergency channel, 121.5. Announce the following:

"Mayday" (three times)
The aircraft number (three times)
Aircraft location as best you know it
Time of day
Altitude
Airspeed and heading
Hours of fuel remaining
A brief description of your emergency
Request for any specific assistance you need.

Repeat this broadcast until a controller or another pilot answers. Most repeater stations need line of sight to make contact, and you may be too low for the signal to get out. If no other aircraft is able to relay your call, climb to a higher altitude until you establish contact, then follow instructions.

Given a choice, all landings should be made into the wind.

All off-airport landings should be made with the master switch off, so there is less danger of fire if the plane gets crunched. Wait until the last moment before you turn it off. When you do switch it off, you will lose radio contact.

One last thing before you land. The mixture control is a red knob, and it should be labeled. It must be pushed all the way in for landings. As soon as the plane is down and stopped, pull the mixture switch all the way back to shut down the engine.

SURVIVAL GEAR

Flying in the North is different than flying anywhere else, whether in air taxis or small private planes. The FAA, in conjunction with the state, issues regulations specific to pilots and passengers. All planes are supposed to carry enough emergency gear to keep them and their passengers alive in remote country where search and rescue might take a while.

During the preflight briefing, the pilot should tell all passengers where the emergency gear is located. If you have questions—how to reach the gear, or what to do with it—ask the pilot before the engine turns over. By law, minimum equipment includes:

- Enough food to sustain everyone onboard for two weeks;
- An axe or hatchet;
- A handgun, shotgun, or rifle with ammunition;
- A knife;

- Two boxes of matches;
- One mosquito head-net for everyone; and
- Two small signaling devices in sealed metal containers.

Between October 15 and April 1, the mandatory equipment list also includes:

- A pair of snowshoes;
- A sleeping bag; and
- A wool blanket for each person older than four years.

The law changes for multi-engine airplanes with a license to carry more than fifteen passengers. Those planes only have to carry food, head-nets, and signal equipment, and, from October 15 to April 1, two sleeping bags and one blanket for every two passengers.

FLAT LIGHT

Flat-light conditions occur when the colors on land match the colors of the sky. You don't have to have snow or wind to have a flat-light occurrence. On an otherwise nice day, fog can settle in or the angle of the sun changes and prevents you from seeing distinguishing characteristics of your surroundings. You lose track of the horizon, affecting your sense of which way is up, and vertigo takes over.

A standard trick is to put something out there you can see to bring the rest of the picture into perspective. A classic example for pilots is to drop spruce boughs out of the plane to bring a landing spot into perspective. The important thing is to remember not to lose sight of your marker.

If you are in a car, pull over until conditions change. Dusk and dawn can create flat light conditions, and you can wait them out.

LANDING ON A STEEP SLOPE

If there is no flat terrain and your only choices are uphill or downhill, land uphill. The center of gravity can change quickly when there is little fuel in the wing tanks, and if you have the fuel, you would be looking farther for a level landing place, right? Be ready to make quick adjustments to changes in weight and wind.

As soon as the wheels touch, add power. Do not touch the brakes.

Keep the plane moving up the hill. Don't let the tail come up. Clearance between the prop and the ground when you're landing uphill is less than on a level landing strip and even a slight nosing over will cause a prop strike.

Keep the power on so the plane won't roll back down the slope. It is not safe to shut down the engine until the wheels are perpendicular to the hill.

Tie the plane, or whatever is left of it, securely. Many planes are blown off hillsides. If there is nothing available to use for ground anchors, fill tie-down bags with rocks. Secure the wings and tail.

DITCHING INTO THE WATER

Aircraft make forced landings on water—a ditching—from time to time. People survive these landings despite the always-cold water and miserable conditions. Here's how to prepare if the engine quits while you are over the water, and you know you are going into the drink:

- Be aware and alert.
- Jettison your doors to reduce buffeting when you hit the water.

- Tighten all seatbelts.
- Tune transponder to 7700.
- Get latitude and longitude numbers from the global positioning system (GPS) and announce them along with your Mayday calls on the radio.

Floatplanes can be unstable on the water in windy conditions. If the wind gets under a wing, the plane can flip over easily. Sometimes a float hits an object under the water, and the plane flips. Regardless of the cause, the result is rapid submersion and disorientation, according to survivors. Even people very familiar with their planes report losing a sense of direction in a cabin underwater.

The body's first reaction to sudden immersion in cold water is the gasp reflex. Resist the reflex if your face is in the water. Use the air in your lungs wisely in the next few seconds. Although it may seem like an eternity, professional rescuers report the average time for underwater egress is five to eight seconds.

Open your eyes. Likely the water will be murky, and the visibility minimal, but what little you see can help you get oriented. Locate a reference point near an exit.

Remember just about anything not attached will float toward the surface.

If you are familiar with the emergency locator transmitter (ELT), make sure it is switched on. It should activate automatically when the plane sustains a blow, but it can malfunction. If the ELT is removable, take it with you.

Take off your headset so you won't get tangled in the cord.

If you are next to an egress window, open it while you still have your seatbelt fastened.

Get a firm handhold on the airframe before you unbuckled your seatbelt. Relocate the reference point.

Unfasten your seatbelt. Pull yourself hand over hand toward the nearest opening. Don't kick while you are still in the aircraft. You could kick other people or tangle your legs in cord and straps.

Kick yourself towards the surface once you are out.

If you are wearing an inflatable vest, pull the cord on your way up.

Survival time in Alaska waters usually is counted in minutes. Once you are out of the airplane, the most serious threat will be hypothermia. You need to reduce the risk of succumbing to it.

If the floats are intact when the plane flips upside down, they will remain buoyant on or near the surface. Climb onto the floats to get out of the water. If you can't climb all the way onto the floats, pull as much of your body out of the water as possible while hanging onto them.

Curl into a fetal position to reduce heat loss from the core areas of your body.

Huddle with other survivors. Keep the smallest people in the center of your huddle.

ON FLOATS

If you have to land a plane on floats, beware of glassy water landings. Smooth water makes it very difficult to judge altitude. Don't stare at the water. Either focus on the far shore or use your peripheral vision to see objects out of the side window as a way to judge your height above the water.

As soon as you touch the water, pull the power all the way back, and apply gentle backpressure on the stick. Release the water rudders so you can steer the plane in the water.

Inexperienced floatplane operators should not try to turn the plane if there is much of a wind. If possible, taxi into the wind until you can beach the plane.

ON SKIS

Choose a frozen lake over a river for your emergency landing. If possible, land close to shore on the leeward side of the lake. Be prepared for rapid deceleration when you touch down, and be ready to push the throttle forward to add a little power. Keep backpressure on the stick or yoke. When you've landed safely, shut the engine down and walk to shore.

While you are setting up to get located and rescued, take the time to prop the skis up on pieces of wood such as saplings or firewood. Friction from the skis melts the snow and the skis then freeze down quickly when the plane isn't moving. It is a tough job to free the plane and when someone rescues you, they will want to get the plane out, too.

FLYING ANIMALS IN A BUSH PLANE

Whether you need to transport an entire dog team, or just a single dog, the logistics are the same. A dog or—heaven forbid—a team of dogs loose in a small aircraft is no joke.

Put the dog in an open feed sack, pull the sack up to the dog's neck, and secure the opening, making sure the dog has room to breath. A dog in a sack will not scratch your face, or jump into the pilot's lap, or do any of the many other destructive things dogs do just to have a good time.

One of the classic Alaska stories, or maybe it's a tale, has to do with a newcomer to sled dog racing who gets his team ready for their first flight to a distant race, but confuses the instructions for bagging his dogs. He tried to put the sack on over the top of the dog's head, succeeding only with the first dog. The rest of the team raised such strong objections that the musher checked with an experienced dog driver to find out the proper way to "bag" his huskies.

Larger animals such as horses should be sedated for a flight. Their owner should be on board as a handler. They should be crated so they can't do harm to the airplane if they start kicking or gnawing on the wiring. It is illegal to fly wolves or bears unless you have a state contract and have been prequalified.

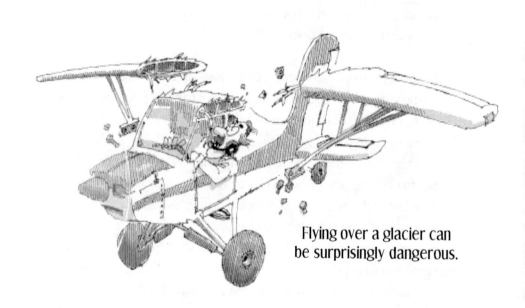

Flying over a glacier can
be surprisingly dangerous.

FLYING OVER GLACIERS

Glaciers can beckon with a siren's call. Alaskans have been landing aircraft on them for decades. Some folks make a living chartering sightseers, mountain climbers, and scientists. Only the best pilots venture on and off glaciers and even with their skills, pilots get into trouble every year.

Some of the unusual factors that can smack a plane out of the sky over glaciers are sudden strong winds including downdrafts and wind shear, flat light conditions, and rapidly deteriorating weather.

Another hazard over glaciers close to population centers is air traffic. Check your Alaska supplement for radio frequency and positions to report. The siren call of a glacier is so much stronger than the whispers of caution that many planes are up there and gawking at the glacier ice when they should spend more time looking for other aircraft in the area.

How and where to cross a river
are important decisions.

Traveling Cross Country

CROSSING RIVERS

Scout it out. Before you venture into a river or creek, make sure you have found the best-possible place to cross. Be patient. This is an important decision.

You are going to get wet, and the water is going to be cold enough to suck the breath out of you, and even push you into hypothermia. Make this crossing as easy on yourself as possible.

Avoid steep cut banks, deadfalls, piles of debris, and bends in the river. Walk upstream to find a shallow crossing. Waves may indicate something below the surface, such as rocks, that you should avoid. Cut a sturdy pole long enough to extend from the ground to the tips of your extended fingers. Use the pole to check of the depth of the river before you step in. Loosen your pack straps so if you are knocked over, you can slide out of it easily. Keep boots or sandals on your feet, but take your outer clothes off and wrap them securely in plastic. (The alternative is to be wet and cold, and have soggy clothes clinging to you. Even if you have a change of clothes, do you want to haul around heavy, wet clothes that are no good to you until they dry out?)

Face the current, feet shoulder apart for solid support. Move the pole, checking the water depth and whereabouts of the bottom. With the pole firmly planted, move one foot toward it. When the foot is planted, move the other foot. Continue across in this manner. Take your time.

If you are wearing hip boots, secure them at the top so water cannot get into them. If you fall over, or the water breaches the tops of your boots, the boots will weigh you down.

If you get knocked down and can't get up, keep your feet pointed downstream and try to maneuver on your back in an effort to stand up again.

Once you are on solid ground, carefully consider your mental state. If you're soggy and unable to think clearly, you are suffering from the onset of hypothermia.

ROPE CROSSING

If several people must cross and you have rope that can reach the width of your crossing, use the rope for an added safety measure. Secure one end to the bank and send the rest of the rope across with the first person. Secure the other end to the opposite shore. You now have a safety line across the river. You can use it as a hand-hold for extra stability and sling packs across on it. (Make certain the rope is securely tied on both ends.) The last one across brings the rope.

RAFTING ACROSS

For light pack loads or people, consider making a raft of heavy branches or small trees. Set two saplings parallel to one another about six feet apart. Lay other saplings across them and lash them securely with cord or rope. If available, a sheet of plastic can be tied down on top. Test the raft to see who or what it will support before you use it to float from one side of the river to the other.

THIN ICE

Winter travel in Alaska is bound to take you across ice. Lakes and rivers become highways for folks on snowmachines, snowshoes, dog teams, skis, and even cars and trucks. Every winter, some of those people go through the ice. In some cases, falling through the ice is a rude awakening. For others it is a tale of adventure. But too often it is a deadly event.

Never trust ice. Big rivers never sleep. Even when the deep cold permeates the air above the ice, water continues to erode it from underneath. An area that is safe one day might be dangerous the next. Safe ice might be just a few feet away from thin ice or open water. Currents, schools of fish, and warm upwellings from hot springs all contribute to thin ice.

Some terrain provides clues to what is happening, unseen, beneath your feet. Narrow areas increase water velocity, which makes for thinner ice as do shoals that extend out from shore. Most rivers in Alaska twist sinuously on their journey to the sea, flowing between steep banks on one side and shallow-sloped sand and gravel bars on the other. Rivers run faster and deeper along high banks than they do along the ırs. So, not only is the ice thinner xt to the high bank, but the water is deeper and swifter as well. Expect thin ice at inlets and outlets, too.

Ice must be at least four inches thick to be safe to support an average-sized adult. But remember it will not be a uniform four inches everywhere you place your foot. You need at least five inches, minimum, for travel on snowmachines and all-terrain vehicles (ATVs). If you're in a car or light pickup truck, you better have at least eight inches, and preferably a foot, of ice to support you.

ICE CLUES

Blue ice is the strongest. Ice bubbles are air pockets that weaken the ice structure. Snow mixed with water as it freezes creates a milky ice, which is weaker than clear blue ice. Snow cover not only keeps you from seeing the ice, but the snow load adds to the weight the ice must bear.

If you are traveling with others, keep your distance. Move single file, a couple of body lengths apart. When you park snowmachines and ATVs, keep them separated by at least ten feet. For obvious reasons, do not allow the weight of the machines and people to be concentrated in one area. Keep in mind that your weight is centered on two small areas where your feet are placed when you are not wearing snowshoes or skis. This is not as safe as when your weight is distributed more widely with snowshoes.

However, when you do break through the ice, you need to get out of your snowshoes quickly. Quick-release bindings can be made from old inner tubes.

Ice picks, or claws, are valuable tools to carry when you travel on ice. You can make them yourself by driving a nail into one end of two four-inch pieces of wood or some other durable material that floats. Sharpen the pointed ends of the nails. Put a hole in the other end of the wood chunks and attach one end of a cord to each chunk.

You may suddenly hear a hollow sound at your feet. This suggests that the water level has dropped below the ice. Stop! Back up slowly. Keep your arms out to break the fall if you go through. Most people go in with little or no warning.

What to do when you fall through: Resist the gasp reflex. Try to stay calm. Turn around to face the direction from which you came. The ice is probably thickest there. If your head is submerged, kick and pull back toward the surface of the water. If your feet touch bottom, push off. Get to the edge of the ice. Stab your ice claws onto the surface ice and pull yourself out as you kick your feet. Back on the surface, stay flat, distribute your weight as wide as possible, and roll or wiggle away from the opening to that you don't break through again. Roll in the snow so that the snow will absorb some of the water soaking your clothes.

If your companion falls through the ice ahead of you: Don't run up to the gaping hole. You won't do him any good if you fall through, too. Call for him to stay calm. Throw a rope. If you don't have a rope, extend whatever you have at hand—a ski pole, a tree branch, a section of sturdy brush. If you must move closer, lie down and wiggle forward.

With enough momentum, snowmachines can skip over patches of open water. But that much momentum means forward motion can carry you under the ice when the machine does sink. Let go as soon as you feel it start to drop.

ATVs' inflated tires will keep the vehicle somewhat buoyant, giving you time to get off the machine, out of the water, and back onto safe ice. Worry about retrieving the ATV later.

Wearing a life jacket under your snowmachine suit keeps you warmer and more buoyant. It is a good idea for everyone who travels on ice to wear a life jacket except for people in an enclosed vehicle. In that situation, you could be too buoyant to get out of the vehicle when it fills with water. To escape a vehicle, lie as flat as possible and pull yourself out a window or windshield, breaking the glass if you need to.

Night travel on ice is not smart. It is easy to outrun your headlights, especially on a fast-moving snowmachine. You or your friends could disappear unnoticed. Open patches of water disappear in the dark. If you must travel at night, slow down and be alert. Check in with everyone in your group on a regular schedule. If possible, wait until the moon is up or the aurora borealis is dancing overhead to provide extra light.

One final piece of advice: Save the alcohol until you are home safe.

BEWARE OF OVERFLOW

Beware of overflow anytime you travel on a lake or river. It can be there, just under the surface, throughout the winter months. Overflow is water seepage that hides beneath the snow on lake or river ice.

An overflow, especially after fresh snowfall, may not be noticed on the frozen surface. Yet, underneath the water can be deep enough to drown in. Even if the overflow area is shallow, an unwary snowshoe hiker or skier quickly can become soaked and covered with slush. The slush can weigh you down and make forward movement impossible. It's thirty below, and you're four miles from the nearest road. Get the picture?

Eventually, the water in an overflow seeps through the insulating layers of ice and snow and freezes. But this might take weeks, and then a new overflow may begin to form over the old one. What this means is that even at the coldest temperatures, there is a chance you will get wet traveling in the boonies.

If the water under the snow is over your head, you may have to swim to safety. The air trapped between the layers of winter clothing helps you to float. Once you are out of the water, you will lose quickly the insulating value of your clothes. Worse yet, they will freeze rapidly and you might find it impossible to move. You must get a fire going and dry your clothes as quickly as possible before you do anything else.

You might hear a soft *whoomp* as the snow settles. This is a clue that you are on or near an overflow. If it has just begun to form, and the snow is several inches deep, you might be able to traverse the area before the water surfaces. Once you have passed over, the water seeps into your tracks and freezes. You have inadvertently made an ice bridge over the gloopy area.

On snowshoes or skis, back track out the way you came in. Once you've returned to a dry surface, remove the snowshoes, and knock off as much of the slush as you can. The blunt side of the hatchet works well for this. Then, prop the equipment up to freeze. When the slush has turned to ice, continue to break it off.

If you boots and pants have gotten wet, walk or roll them in dry snow. This acts as a sponge and may wick out layers of water. If you are soaked through, it is time to make a fire and dry out.

On a snowmachine, once you get out of the overflow, prop the front end up so you can get the slush off the skis and the track. Backtrack to get out unless you know the overflow area is small and you can power through it.

Once you get bogged down in the middle of the overflow, you are going to have to get wet to get free. You want to avoid this!

ICEBERGS & GLACIER FACES

There is a strong temptation to get close to a glacier face, to get a photo of you next to a towering mountain of ice. This temptation can be stronger than the survival instinct. Don't give in to the temptation.

Glacier faces calve continually and unpredictably. This means that tons of ancient ice can drop on you at any moment. It will be a quick death, but messy and perhaps dangerous for the search and rescue folks who have to recover your smushed body. How rude!

Icebergs look deceptively small because you don't see what all you get. Something like ninety percent of the berg is under water being eroded by the sea. And when the bottom gets eroded enough to become lighter than the top, the iceberg flips. Like a glacier calving, this is not a predictable occurrence. It happens fast and without warning. Stay off the icebergs no matter what supermodels you see posing on one in a TV commercial. And don't put your tongue on one either.

Bergy bits are small chunks of ice, a perfect size for the cooler. But once again, they are bigger than what you see and heavier than you think. If you decide to net one to cool down the day's catch or cool a refreshing beverage, look for the smallest ones you can find. Tell the others in your party what you are doing. Wear your life jacket. Be prepared to let go of the net if the weight is suddenly too much for you to lift. Your goal is to bring the bit on board, not to fall in after it.

You may have to improvise to attract the
attention of search planes.

Lost or Stranded

SIGNALING FOR RESCUE

Picture this: You are out in the middle of nowhere or on a remote coastline, lost or stranded. What next?

First, know that if a formal search is underway, searchers may look for you during hours of darkness. They may use infrared-sensitive detectors that respond to heat and light.

If you hear an aircraft nearby, discharge your flare gun, if you have one, or create a vertical red line pointing straight up with your laser pointer. These signals may be seen from as far away as five miles. Do not point either directly at an aircraft.

If you have an analog ELT, know that its battery should last about one hundred hours. Place it as high as possible, with the antenna in a vertical position. Putting it on a metal surface including a wing or wing rib will increase its transmitting ability. It is not necessary to keep the battery warm. Don't hold the ELT against your body, as your body will absorb most of the signal energy. High-altitude aircraft can hear an ELT as far away as one hundred miles. You might want to delay turning it on until you hear aircraft overhead, but make sure you turn it on within the first twenty-four hours of a forced landing.

If there are no fuel leaks, turn on the master switch of your boat or plane. Turn on the plane's radio, set to 121.5, and listen for the ELT signal to make sure it is working. Turn off the radio and the master switch. If the weather is cold, keep the battery wrapped for warmth, turning it on only when you hear another aircraft.

You may have to improvise if you didn't bring one of the many devices now on the market to signal for a rescue. Fire and smoke are useful signals. Use extreme caution that your fire does not spread. Smoke is the better signal on a clear, calm day, while fire naturally is more likely to be seen at night. Gather materials that can make a smoky fire—rubber parts from the aircraft, oil, green boughs, or moss—and be ready to use them when you hear a search plane.

Shiny objects such as aluminum foil can be put out to attract attention to your camp.

MAKING SNOWSHOES

Snowshoes are easier to craft than skis, don't require special footwear, and are far superior to skis for breaking trail. It takes time, effort, and patience to make even a crude pair of snowshoes. Before starting, put your energy first into making a shelter. Once you are hunkered down and rested, you can decide if you need to travel to assist in your own rescue.

If you have to travel a good distance—at least several miles—through snow deeper than ten inches, making snowshoes is worth your time. Snowshoes don't allow you to float on top of the snow, but provide a stable platform for your feet you from slogging and slipping. You defini better time with them. Wearing snowshoes c your body's energy and reduces the chance of ankle or worse injuries.

The best trailbreaker is a person with lor legs and good lungs. Breaking trail in dee snow can be exhausting. Two or more peop should trade off taking the lead. Don't overc it trying to carry a heavy load while al breaking trail. Let somebody behind you carry the heavier load. If you're alone, you may have to move your load in stages, backtracking on your newly broken trail.

But travel as light as you can. Rest often. Don't allow yourself to become exhausted.

Survival snowshoes don't have to look great. They only have to support you. Here's how to make a pair:

1. Use green (living) saplings thin enough to bend and thick enough to remain strong and not break.

2. Bend one long sapling back onto itself and fasten the ends together to form a tail.

3. Attach a piece of green wood for a horizontal brace one-third of the way up from the tail, and another piece one-third of the way back from the toe.

4. Use cord, twine, wire, or rawhide strips from animal skins to lace the snowshoes.

5. Make a thick and durable horizontal lacing below the toe brace. The ball of your foot pivots on this lace and should have just enough space to clear the front brace.

6. Attach the lacing to the sides of the snowshoe and to the front horizontal brace, which will frame your foot.

7. If you are short on lacing material, conserve it by filling in the snowshoe in the following order:

- In the center of the snowshoe, weave lacings horizontally and vertically.
- Fill in the area from the toe to the front brace.
- Fill in the area from the tail to the back brace.

With the ball of your foot on the primary horizontal lacing, attach the snowshoes to your feet with cloth bindings, strips of rubber, or the same cord you used to make the webbing.

A balanced snowshoe and binding allows your foot to pivot on the lace toe to heel in a normal step. When you pick up your foot, the tail of the snowshoe should trail diagonally, tail towards the ground. Adjust your foot bindings until the snowshoes balance properly.

SURVIVAL FOOD

You are alone, far from anywhere and feeling weak from hunger. When you reach into your cache of survival foods, what will you find? If you packed tasty, tempting foods, there is a good chance you or one of those people who say they are your friends will have eaten part or all of the stash already. That's why Alaska off-road racers packed high-quality dog food.

In addition to making sure the survival foods are kept dry, don't melt in the heat, and are edible in the coldest temperatures, you need to keep them safe from casual nibblers. The best way to do this is to test for taste before hand.

Some people go so far as relying on dog biscuits for emergency food, believing no one will chow down on them before it is absolutely necessary. While you might not want to go to that extreme, you can use the idea as a gold standard for taste when you are trying out nutritious foods for your cache. Remember, too, that dog biscuits are meant to be chewed to clean dogs' teeth and are not a good survival food.

Some of the best foods are lightweight and packed with nutrition such as salmon strips, jerky, and pemmican. The old staple, pilot bread, is just a white-flour cracker, but it is more durable than regular crackers, doesn't mold like regular bread does, and will fill you up quickly. It goes well with peanut butter, dried meats, and fish. But don't expect to get enduring energy from it.

LISTEN FOR YOUR SUPPER

You might be low on grub, with no quick way to turn some critter into lunch. But all you really need to do is listen. Somewhere, every day, bears, and wolves kill moose, caribou, and each other. They probably didn't eat their kill all in one sitting.

Ravens know all about the kills and they talk a lot. Ravens don't like to eat alone. Every meal is a party. Listen for their squawking invitation to a feast. Look for them in the sky. Follow your eyes and ears. As you get closer to the carcass, slow down. Don't spook the ravens until you have the location pinpointed. Make sure the area is bear-free for the moment. If the ravens are still around, you should find some meat still clinging to the bones. Take advantage of a free meal, just like the ravens.

Be aware of highways seasonally
prone to avalanches.

Disasters (Natural)

AVALANCHES

Avalanches are the natural result of erosion, weathering, and gravity on the snow pack. Unlike earthquakes, avalanches are fairly predictable because we know what conditions most likely will cause them. On slopes as slight as fifteen degrees, fresh snow on top of a packed layer of old snow could rupture. As the degree of slope increases, so does the risk of avalanche.

The most dangerous time for people traveling the backcountry is when the air temperatures warm up after a fresh snowfall. Climbers, skiers, and snow-boarders have triggered avalanches. Increasingly snow machine dudes have caused avalanches by "high-marking." (See "high-marking," Page 123.)

Rescue beacons, shovels, level-headed traveling companions, and cell phones all have saved people who were buried. Remember that the survival rate drops to less than forty percent after a victim has been buried for twenty minutes. If traveling in avalanche country, you should carry a search probe and shovel, as well as transceiver. It's also important that members in the party know how to use a transceiver and have practiced doing so.

Several highways and populated areas are prone to avalanches. Several areas of Juneau, the state capitol, lie at the bottom of well-known avalanche chutes. Avalanches closed the Seward Highway for much of the winter of 1999-2000. It is not uncommon for snow slides to interrupt traffic on the Glenn and lower Richardson highways.

Stay on the windward side of the slope when traveling through mountains in the backcountry. Snow and ice cornices build up on the leeward side. Back away from visible fractures in the snow. Restrict your travel to the cooler times of the day. The danger is greatest when the temperature is at or near its daily high.

If you hear rumbling, or feel the ground shaking, run laterally away from the direction of the slide. You will not be able to outrun an avalanche, but you might be able to get out of its path. Swaths of trees may help break up the snow slide and give you a bit of protection.

If you are on skis or snowshoes, be aware of the subtle changes around you. Hollow-sounding snow, or snow that feels stiff, are clues to impending avalanches. Chances are slim that you will take a direct hit and thank goodness for that, because avalanches are powerful enough to destroy buildings and toss cars around like toys.

If you find yourself caught in the rush of snow, use your arms and legs as if you were swimming or paddling a kayak. Keep up this movement as long as you can. The idea is to give yourself breathing room if you are buried or, better yet, keep part of your body on top of the snow.

EARTHQUAKES

In an average day, some part of Alaska is rocking and rolling every hour or two. The state experiences about five thousand earthquakes each year, or an average of nearly fifteen quakes every day, according to the Geophysical Institute at the University of Alaska Fairbanks.

Three of the six most powerful earthquakes ever recorded occurred in Alaska, the biggest of them being the Good Friday Earthquake that registered 9.2 on the Richter scale on March 28, 1964.

Almost any given place in Alaska "is eventually going to experience heavy shaking" is the warning from the Joint Commission for Alaska Federal-State Land-Use Planning.

So, have we gotten your attention yet?

Here's what you can do to protect yourself when the ground starts moving.

INSIDE

Take cover under a sturdy piece of furniture or a doorway. (But avoid metal doorways.) Stay away from windows, heavy objects that might fall, and anywhere where fuel or combustible material might catch fire or explode.

OUTSIDE

Move away from buildings to avoid falling debris. Be aware of, and get away from, power lines, light poles, and tall trees.

When the shaking stops: Shut off the gas and oil lines. Turn off the electrical breakers. Do not light matches or lighters until you are sure there are no leaking fumes. Check for injuries and give as much aid as possible without moving seriously injured people unless absolutely necessary. Be prepared for more shaking from aftershocks.

The water in your hot-water heater and in your toilet tank can be used for drinking.

FLOODS

Some floods in Alaska are predictable. Ice jams during spring breakup cause rivers to back up rapidly. August, the wet month, is also the time of year when most glacial melt is at its peak, so rivers are full to overflowing. A less-predictable flood is caused by glacial dams breaking free.

Soil in Alaska is mostly shallow and much of it is easily saturated because of the underlying permafrost.

When you monitor the radio, remember that a flood watch means that flood is possible while a warning means that a flood already is occurring, or will soon.

Before heading out into the backcountry, understand the potential for flooding by knowing what the weather has been for the previous couple of weeks and the propensity of nearby rivers to flood. If hard rains fall for a few hours, or if it rains steadily for a few days, prepare for a flood. Be aware that if you are camping in a low-lying drainage area that heavy rains upriver can push flood water to your camp even if the local weather is benign.

If you are camping on a river, look closely at the vegetation for debris from earlier floods. Previous high-water marks are evident by old grasses, twigs, and branches washed into standing brush. Pitch your tent on higher ground.

Create a measuring stick by cutting notches every one or two inches and then pound the stick into the mud at the water's edge. The rise of the water will tell you if it's time to move camp.

Driving an ATV or a car, do not cross water if you can't see the bottom. It takes only about two feet of water to float a car and less than that for ATVs. If you chose to drive across a flooded area and the vehicle stalls, abandon it and move to high ground.

FLOODS AT HOME

If you are in a home threatened by flood, move valuables to the highest floor. Prepare to evacuate and take valuable documents with you.

During the 1967 flood in Fairbanks, some homeowners learned the potential hazard of trying to keep their basements dry by sandbagging. The floodwater created hydrostatic pressure, which meant the water outside sought to equalize the pressure inside. It can implode your foundation. A better strategy is to fill your basement with clean water to equalize the pressures, keeping the filthy flood water outside and possibly saving your furnace.

See the section Traveling Cross Country, page 81 for advice on traveling in floodwaters.

TSUNAMIS

If you are in a coastal area, expect a tsunami after any earthquake strong enough to be felt. Chunks of land can be knocked loose underwater, creating waves that can travel 400 miles per hour. Of the 125 deaths reported in Alaska after the 1964 Earthquake, 110 resulted from tsunamis. An estimated 520,000 square kilometers were displaced vertically, and the resulting waves killed an additional fifteen people as far away as California and Hawaii. Sometimes there is a noticeable change in water levels before a tsunami hits, but not always.

When the ground shakes: If you are in a low-lying area along the coast, run or drive immediately to higher ground. If you can't get to high ground, holding on to a big, heavy object is a better option than doing nothing. The highest wave on record was 220 feet at Shoup Bay near Valdez after the '64 quake. Whatever you do, do not go down to a beach to watch for a tsunami.

If you are in a boat: A boat in a harbor is not safe. If possible, head out to deep water at full speed. In the open ocean, the wave will be a harmless swell that runs under the boat.

When you are on safe ground: Wait for an all-clear signal. If a wave hits, expect more to follow. Keep in mind that the first wave may not be the biggest. It may be necessary to stay put for up to twenty-four hours after a wave hits. Many people have been killed because they went down to the shore to get a better look. Big mistake.

VOLCANOES

Western coastal areas are part of the Ring of Fire encircling the Pacific Ocean and are home to active volcanoes.

The 1,550-mile-long Aleutian Chain, the Alaska Peninsula, Kodiak Island, and Cook Inlet all have been covered with ash following volcanic eruptions. The Wrangell Mountains in the southeastern part of the Alaska mainland also are volcanically active.

There have been some big blowouts in recent years with ash plumes that shut down air traffic. Mount Redoubt was active enough to cause various disruptions in 1989 and 1990. Mt. Spur dumped ash on Anchorage in 1992. The explosion of Katmai in 1912 created the Valley of Ten Thousand Smokes and ranked as the world's largest eruption of the Twentieth Century. In addition to all this activity in Alaska, the Kamchatka Peninsula to the west in Siberia is volcanically active and is capable of dumping ash on Alaska with the prevailing winds.

The Alaska Volcano Observatory color-codes the smokers much along the same lines as the colors used by the U.S. Department of Homeland Security.

When you're in the middle of ash fall:

- Stay indoors, bring the pets in, and close the doors, windows and any other openings to the outdoors such as vents and chimney flues.
- Turn off and cover electronic equipment.

Western Alaska is part
of the volcanic Ring of Fire.

- Seal computer disks, memory cards, and other small electronics in plastic bags.
- Have a battery-powered radio handy in case you lose power.

If you're driving:
- Secure a hose stocking over the carburetor intake as an extra protection against gritty ash.
- Keep your headlights on.
- Use the wipers in combination with the windshield washer.
- Slow down. The ash can be slippery.

If you have to go outdoors, wear a respirator. Make sure the children's respirators fit them properly. Consider wearing eye protection, too.

Remember that the ash is very heavy. It won't take much accumulation to sink boats and bust airplane wings, so keep them cleared off. This goes for flat roofs as well.

To clean up when it is over, use a vacuum for everything from floors to furniture to pets. Ash is very abrasive. Wiping it off can scratch and gouge.

Change the oil, oil filters, and air filters in all engines.

Eventually migrant birds
will bring in the avian flu.

Disasters (Self Inflicted)

DISEASE AND ILLNESS

In Alaska's recent history, Native populations have been decimated by diseases introduced by gold seekers, fur traders, whalers, and missionaries, to name a few sources. But new diseases will find a way to Alaska soon, according to predictions from public health officials.

Because Alaska is a destination for migrant birds seeking nesting grounds, it may be one of the first places avian flu shows up. More birds were tested in Alaska (17,023 in 2006) than in the rest of the United States. For more information, find National Avian Influenza Surveillance Information at http://wildlifedisease.nbii.gov/ai/

Alaska has some superb medical care, especially in the cities. But most villages have at best a public health aid and top of the line medical care is an hours-long flight away.

If you are going to travel a less-beaten path, be prepared to handle your health care needs. This means, for starters, whatever medicine you require and a good first-aid kit.

The federal Centers for Disease Control suggest you may want to take along some if not all of these items:

MEDICATIONS

Personal prescription medications in their original containers (copies of all prescriptions should be carried, including the generic names for medications, and a note from the prescribing physician on letterhead stationery for controlled substances and injectable medications)

- Anti-malarial medications, if applicable

- Over-the-counter anti-diarrheal medication (e.g., bismuthsubsalicylate, loperamide)

- Antibiotic for self-treatment of moderate to severe diarrhea

- Antihistamine

- Decongestant, alone or in combination with antihistamine

- Anti-motion sickness medication

- Acetaminophen, aspirin, ibuprofen, or other medication for pain or fever

- Mild laxative

- Cough suppressant/expectorant

- Throat lozenges

- Antacid

- Antifungal and antibacterial ointments or creams

- One percent hydrocortisone cream

- Epinephrine auto-injector (e.g., EpiPen), especially if history of severe allergic reaction. Also available in smaller-dose package for children.

Other Important Items

- Insect repellent containing DEET® (up to 50%)

- Sunscreen (preferably SPF 15 or greater)

- Aloe gel for sunburns

- Digital thermometer

- Oral rehydration solution packets

- Basic first-aid items (adhesive bandages, gauze, ace wrap, antiseptic, tweezers, scissors, cotton-tipped applicators)

- Antibacterial hand wipes or alcohol-based hand sanitizer containing at least 60% alcohol

- Moleskin for blisters

- Lubricating eye drops

- First-aid quick reference card

Last but not least
Other items that may be useful in certain circumstances:

- Mild sedative or other sleep aid

- Anti-anxiety medication

- High-altitude preventive medication

- Water purification tablets

- Commercial suture/syringe kits

- Latex condoms

BOTULISM

Botulism is most commonly associated with the west and southwest coastal areas of Alaska where traditional Native foods include seal, salmon eggs, whitefish, salmon heads, and beaver tail.

Botulism is not found in home-canned foods, but it has been found in drying foods, even with salt brine; rendered seal oil; and "stinky" foods. Stinky foods were traditionally made by burying meats, eggs, or fish in a clay-lined pit in the ground to ferment for a couple of weeks. Today, plastic or glass often is used instead of clay, and the containers might be left above ground. Some researchers suspect that the warmer temperatures associated with above-ground fermentation contribute to an increase in the number of botulism spores. Another unconfirmed suspicion is that regular consumption of these foods can build up resistance in a body. So, if you are not used to eating stinky foods, you might fall ill while regular consumers remain unaffected.

Seek medical help immediately if you have any gastrointestinal illness along with blurred vision, muscular weakness, dry throat, or inability to swallow after eating suspected foods.

Although the total number of cases increased over the decades from the first documented case in the 1950s, the increase might represent not additional cases but more people reporting the illness and seeking treatment for it. The number of fatalities has declined. Although official confirmation of botulism is available only from the Centers for Disease Control in Atlanta, Georgia, village health aids are well trained to recognize the symptoms.

CRUISE SHIP OUTBREAK

Every summer, it seems at least one group tour or cruise has an outbreak of those ever-popular gastrointestinal diseases. According to the Centers for Disease Control, gastroenteritis is an inflammation of the stomach and small and large intestines. Viral gastroenteritis is an infection caused by a variety of viruses that result in vomiting or diarrhea. It is often called the "stomach flu," although it is not caused by the influenza viruses.

In 2007, according to the state of Alaska, about sixty percent of Alaska's 1.7 million visitors arriving between May and September were cruise-ship passengers. The chances of getting sick on an Alaska cruise are slim, but that's little comfort to someone whose vacation of a lifetime turns into living hell. According to the CDC, here are a few common-sense steps you can take to avoid illness on a cruise:

1. Wash your hands thoroughly and vigorously with soap before and after eating or smoking, after touching your face, after going to the bathroom, and—duh!—when your hands are dirty.

2. Leave the area if you see someone get sick (vomiting or diarrhea). Report sickness, yours or others, to the cruise staff. Keep in mind you can become sick if you ingest contaminated particles that travel through the air.

3. Take care of yourself. Get plenty of rest, drink lots of water. Resting helps rebuild your immune system. Drinking water helps prevents dehydration.

4. Be considerate of other people's health. If you're ill before taking a cruise, call the cruise line to find out about options to reschedule.

For more information about viral outbreaks aboard ships, visit **http://www.cdc.gov/ncidod/dvrd/revb/gastro/faq.htm**. Learn more about CDC's Vessel Sanitation Program: **http://cdc.gov/nceh/vsp/**

FASHION FAUX PAS

Fashion in Alaska is almost an oxymoron. You may see people trying to walk on snow and ice in slick-soled shoes, even high heels, in urban parts of the state. But these fashion statements can kill you once you step outside the city limits.

SHOES

Although the usual soft-soled athletic shoe is as popular in Alaska as anywhere else, geographic regions and seasons determine footgear of people who work outside. In Southeast, the Aleutian Chain, and other coastal areas, workers wear rubber boots much of the year. In the Interior, hip boots are for summer, felt packs or Bunny boots are for winter, and rubber boots are for breakup. Rubber boots should be large enough to allow you to wear a couple pair of socks. Caribou mukluks are worn in wintertime in the northern villages.

CLOTHING

Southeast and the Aleutian Chain are where "best dressed" means rain pants, hooded rain jackets, and rubber gloves with grips on the fingers. In winter, layers of long underwear and sweaters underneath the rain gear will help you endure the weather. Insulated overalls are standard, too.

HATS AND GLOVES

Away from the coast, where the weather is drier, fur hats and fur ruffs on parkas have kept many generations of Alaskans warm in the cold months. Mittens may be trimmed in fur, too, and they will be big enough to accommodate several pair of liners. The fur on the back of your mittens is a nose warmer. And if you don't have anyone to tell you the color and condition of your nose, make sure you hold your mitten up to it every ten minutes or so to ward off frostbite. Fine motor coordination is something that falls by the wayside when you're wearing gloves.

Occasionally, you may need something fancy. For example, a semi-formal event is a time to spiff up a bit. The general understanding is that you will try to get most of the dog hairs off your clothes.

The savvy person will have the standby clothes, the ones that you keep you warm and dry, stashed in their vehicle on the way to and from any gala bash. If you have an accident, or your car breaks down, you will need to make a quick change to get into something more functional. Otherwise, you might lose your toes to frostbite as you change the flat tire or wait for help.

Here's the secret to "dressing up" in Alaska. You will always be considered adequately dressed for any occasion if you wear mostly clean jeans and flannels.

For the most part, Alaska ignores fashion. If you are intrigued by Alaskans' unconventional attitudes about fashion and etiquette, you may enjoy *Fashion Means Your Fur Hat is Dead*, a book by Mike Doogan.

HIGH MARKING

High marking is a fairly recent fad. It means driving your snowmachine as high as possible up a vertical slope of a mountainside before your machine loses forward momentum, at which point you slide or topple back down. It is a good way to trigger avalanches that can wipe you and your friends off the face of the mountain. What fun, huh?

If you are eager for a winter outdoor adventure with an element of risk and your newfound friends suggest high marking, should you say yes? Absolutely not. You would be amazed by the number of people killed or injured playing dangerous games with their snowmachines each winter.

Although you may be smart enough not to take up high marking, not everyone is. Keep an eye out for other folks trying this out, especially if they are traveling above you. Avoid them and live longer.

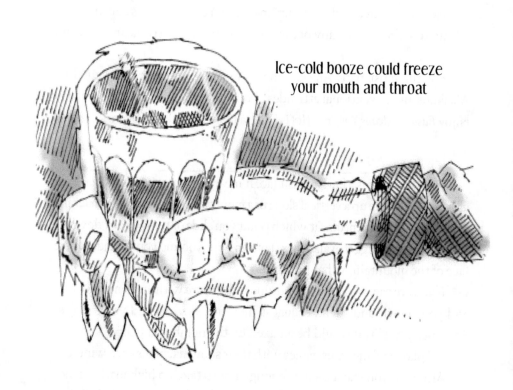

Ice-cold booze could freeze
your mouth and throat

ICE-COLD BOOZE

The image of the weary winter traveler taking a long pull on a bottle of booze at the end of a long day on the trail is enduring in literature and film. But nowadays almost everyone knows—or should know—the down side of adding alcohol to a survival situation. You make your own choices.

The important thing to remember is that at sub-freezing temperatures, any liquid that has not frozen in the bottle due to its alcohol content will be at ambient temperature when the hootch goes down the hatch. This is a time-honored way to freeze your mouth and throat. If in doubt, test a drop on your hand or finger before you take a belt.

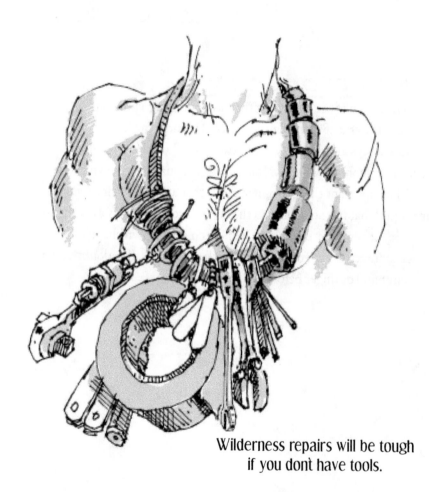

Wilderness repairs will be tough
if you don't have tools.

Things That Need Fixing

CHAINSAWS

When a chainsaw starts, runs, and then dies after a short time in cold weather, check to see if a screen covers the exhaust vent. This screen is a spark arrester, installed so you won't accidentally start a forest fire with an exhaust spark. In cooler weather, the exhaust is thick enough to coat the screen and smother the engine. Remove the screen, and the chainsaw should continue to run.

SMALL ENGINES

Small engines are the lifeblood of travel in Alaska. Boats with outboard motors, snowmachines, and all-terrain vehicles are important means of transport. We must depend on them, especially if we are in the backcountry. These machines are more tools than toys in Alaska.

Small engines don't necessarily mean small prices. Even if you have the bucks to get someone to fix your dead or dying rig, the nearest repair shop may be many miles away over rough terrain. Your choice may be to fix the machine or build an emergency shelter and hunker down to await rescue.

As I've said, keep your pockets loaded with survival gear specific to your mode of travel and your geographic region. Maybe you are a whiz at repairing engines in a shop with a full set of tools and manuals. But when your engine gives up the ghost in Alaska, the odds are good that your hands will be stiff with cold before the repair is finished. Or that you will be sucked dry by mosquitoes. You wouldn't have a manual. It might be dark or getting dark. Unless you prefer to wait for rescue, you'll have to make repairs, even if only temporary, and limp home.

In addition to the usual list of survival supplies, add a spark plug, a spare belt, and bailing wire. If you don't want to carry a sparkplug feeler gage, set the gap on the plug before you leave home. Know how much fuel you will need to get where you are going. If it will not fit in the tank, you need to carry spare fuel containers. If your engine has fuses, carry a couple of spares. Of course, we all know that no Alaskan leaves home without a roll of Duct Tape.

Check your fuel before you leave home. Like fine wine, it doesn't last forever. It should smell like gasoline. If it has been exposed to air for a long time, it will pick up impurities and smell sour. Drain it and get fresh fuel.

Make sure you have the right mix ratio of oil to gas, if your machine takes its fuel mixed instead of straight up.

If your machine has been running and dies, keep in mind that the engine is hot. If you spill gas or oil, the still-hot engine could be a source of ignition.

The first thing to check on a dead engine is the fuel tank. No fuel means you might have an easy solution to your problem, if you brought a supply with you.

If you have fuel and the engine still doesn't start, check your spark plug. If you can see carbon fouling, rust, or wear, replace the plug with the one in your pocket. If you didn't set the proper gap before you took off on this adventure, do it before you attach the plug. Most small engine plugs should be gapped anywhere from 0.03 to 0.04 inches.

Test the ignition. Make sure all the surfaces are free of gas and oil. With the spark plug hex end grounded on the bare metal of the engine, pull the starter rope or turn the ignition keep. You should see a blue spark arc across the plug gap. That spark means you have ignition.

If you have no ignition, look carefully for shorted or broken wires. You might have to tug gently on the wires to know for sure. Wrap a shorted wire with Duct Tape. If you find a broken wire, peel back the insulation on each end of the break until about a half inch of bare wire shows. Twist the bare ends together and tape them with Duct Tape.

If the machine still does not start, look at the fuel shut-off valve to make sure it was not closed inadvertently. Check the fuel line to make sure it is not plugged or broken. If it is plugged, remove one end and ream the clots out with a length of wire such as the wire tie from your bag of Pilot Bread. Check the fuel cap and clear it of gook if necessary. Also check the fuel filter for big hunks of debris that can clog the flow.

If your engine sputters, surges, or runs only on choke, and you have a float style carburetor, it's a good bet you have a stuck or flooded float bowl. Turn the fuel shut-off valve to OFF. Loosen the nut at the bottom of the carburetor. Let the gas drain out. When the gas has drained, remove the bowl. Don't let the float swing all the way down. The nut should have two tiny holes. Make sure they are clear. Ream them out with a thin wire. Wipe the bowl clean. Gently move the float up and down. If it feels heavy, or you can tell fluid is sloshing around in it, remove the float. Try to drain it. Don't put another hole in it. If you can see the hole where the fuel leaked in, patch the hole temporarily with tape, spruce sap or—if you brought it with you—metal mender.

If you have a diaphragm in the carburetor instead of a float, inspect the needle valve and seat for grit and dirt. Clear it out. Make sure the vent hole is clear. Make sure the inlet control lever lies parallel with the diaphragm housing. Gently bend it into place if necessary.

If the engine backfires often, it can be a sign the compression is low. Low compression is not going to be fixed on the trail. Plan ahead. The engine could die soon.

Remember that in cold weather, breather tubes and vent holes frost over quickly. Know where they are so you can do a quick check and clear them as needed.

Be aware that most people who die in ATV and snowmachine accidents in Alaska have been drinking. Alcohol slows reactions, clouds judgment, and heightens the body's susceptibility to hypothermia. The next critical killing factor is running the machines in the dark, which is most of the time in winter. Open water, obstructions, and other dangers can't be seen until it is too late.

Know where you are going and how long you should be gone. Give your itinerary to a responsible person, even if you have to spend hours finding one—a responsible person, that is. Joke. When your machine is busted beyond your ability to repair it, make camp. Stay warm. Make certain your campsite is visible from the air and surrounding terrain.

PLUMBING DISASTERS

Many people in Alaska live without plumbing. Hauling water and using an outhouse are everyday occurrences. When temperatures drop, things don't change much for these folks. But when you have running water, you goal is to keep it running within the pipes, all year. This can be easier said than done in Alaska conditions.

The most likely places for pipes to freeze are where they enter or leave the house, or in a wall where the insulation is thin. The second most likely place is under ground, and the most likely time for underground pipes to freeze, believe it or not, is when the temperatures rise and drive the frost deeper.

You can add insulation to problem areas or create a safe external source of heat nearby. Outside, snow is a good insulator for buried pipes. If the snowfall is too little or too late, pile straw on top of the buried lines.

If you have ice in the lines, you will hear it as a chunky rattle when the water is running. When you hear that, run as much water as you can to keep the line clear. Do laundry, take a shower, do the dishes. Once you're caught up with the chores, run water into containers. Then, you will have water if the pipe freezes. Some folks leave a faucet or two open slightly during very cold weather. This can keep the line from freezing solid or, at worst, let you know when the problem is getting worse.

If you catch not-yet-frozen pipes right away, before the ice expands and breaks the lines, use a hair dryer, or a heating pad for thawing. Don't let the pipes get too hot to touch. Keep the hair dryer in motion along the pipe. If you chose to use a heat source such as a propane or white-gas heater, do not leave it unattended. More than a few Alaskans have burned down their homes while trying to thaw a pipe.

WHAT TO DO IF THE PIPES ARE FROZEN SOLID

If the water is frozen solid in the pipes, gather your wits and tools before you tackle this problem. If you are lucky, the expansion of the water into ice will have ruptured just the joints, not the pipe itself.

At the very least, you will need flux, solder, a saws-all, and some channel locks. Listen as well as look for water once things begin to thaw. You may have to knock holes in the walls to get to the broken pipes.

If you are not up to dealing with this disaster yourself, call in a professional. Unfortunately critical problems such as furnace failures or frozen pipes tend to occur at forty below zero in the middle of the night on a Sunday or holiday. Plumbers, like snowplow drivers, electricians, and other skilled workers who make home visits, enjoy cookies and a hot drink.

Extra lights can
push away the blues during
the dark months.

Weather & Seasonal Weirdness

COLD TEMPERATURE CAUTIONS

Global warming will seem more like a theory than relative north of the Alaska Range in the wintertime. Anticipate temperatures of thirty degrees below zero. And that's just the start of seriously cold weather. Typically the temperature has to drop another ten to twenty degrees before school and public events are cancelled. But life goes on and you should remember a few things to keep severe weather from getting the best of you.

At severe sub-zero temperatures, the air has virtually no moisture, and you can frost your lungs by breathing deeply in the cold. Use a scarf or facemask to block the cold air, warming it and adding a little moisture before it reaches your sinuses.

If you have latchkey kids, have a back-up plan of where they can go to be safe and warm in case they lose the key. Don't let the kids run to the school bus. Don't let them wait too long for the bus. And, obviously, overcome their casual attitude about clothing and make them dress properly for the cold.

Propane begins to gel at forty below, but do not use a heater or heating blanket on the tank. Doing so could cause expansion when the propane begins to flow to the stove again, resulting in a fireball in the kitchen.

Fuel oil begins to gel at sixty below, but if the line to the house is buried deep enough you should still have flow. If the fuel line is not buried, insulate it with straw bales before the snow flies and temperatures fall in the fall.

Doors warp in extreme cold, and you might not be able to lock your house during a cold spell. Lock windows to make sure they don't pop open in the cold.

Fan belts can become brittle and snap easily in very low temperatures. Make sure your belt is in good shape in the fall. That's the time to replace a worn-out belt as part of your winterization routine. When you replace a belt, wrap a spare just behind it under the hood so you will have a belt ready to slide into place, if needed.

Have cash for a taxicab on hand, and be prepared to wait your turn for the next cab. During cold weather, everyone has car troubles at the same time. For the same reason, tow trucks will be hard to come by, and automotive repair shops will be swamped.

Double-check your garage door when you leave. If you forget to close it, you may come home to a frozen boiler, frozen water pipes, and a very cold house. If this happens, you might get the furnace going again simply by hitting the reset button on the furnace. If this doesn't work, you would be wise to call a professional to thaw the house.

It can be tempting not to dress for the cold thinking you are stepping out of the office for just a minute or two to get the mail, pick up the newspaper, or visit the outhouse. But if you lock yourself out and are wearing only your robe, slippers, and the smile you were born with, you could freeze to death. Resist the temptation! Dress for the weather.

WHITEOUT & FOG

It sounds pretty, but if you are caught unaware, a whiteout can be deadly. Fog, blowing snow, haze, and smoke all can cause a sudden loss of visibility. With no horizon you have no way to tell which way is up, down, or sideways. Your mind may tell you it knows the way to stay upright, but it is almost always wrong. Human minds need visual clues to stay oriented.

Haze and smoke conditions can come quickly in the summer. Haze is always worse near sources of moisture. Forest fires burn chunks of Alaska every summer. Afternoon cumulus clouds build up and throw out a whopping number of lightning strikes, and smoke from fires obscures what had been a clear sky. Fog can form anytime of the year, but is mostly likely in the warmer months. Blowing snow not only obscures your vision, but snow-covered terrain adds to the flat light effect and disorients you quickly. (See Flat Light, page 70.)

In a car, if you can't see the road, let alone the horizon, pull over and stop. Tie a bright flag or shiny object on your antenna to make your car visible to snowplow operators and other motorists. If blowing snow causes a whiteout, and you are running the engine to stay warm, make sure the exhaust pipe remains clear of snow. Otherwise, carbon monoxide poisoning could kill you.

Many places in Alaska will have poor or no radio reception, so you may not be able to get weather updates. Pile all the spare clothes you have in the car. Cover up in a spare sleeping bag that is part of your winter car gear. Keep your body warm with light exercise and periodic stretching. Be glad you packed not-so-tasty snacks and plenty of water to keep your energy up.

Ice fog is a common winter condition in cold weather in urban areas. You will find that it is thicker than ordinary fog. Slow down! A combination of ice fog and icy roads can be destructive and dangerous, as a few Fairbanks drivers discover (or rediscover) every winter with the arrival of ice fog. Once you get out of town, or climb in elevation, you will leave the ice fog behind.

In an airplane, avoid whiteout conditions, if you are not equipped with instruments and training on them to get behind visual navigation. When you see the weather start to come down to minimums, find a place to land. Or, if you have enough fuel and know the weather is clear behind you, turn around, and go back. You also can get on the radio to find out what the weather is ahead of you, but it is not a good idea to rely on remote sensors in the belief you can fly on instruments for just a few minutes and get through the whiteout conditions.

If you are suddenly caught unaware in clouds or smoke: Fly straight and level and slow down. Keep your head movements to a minimum and a light touch on the stick and rudders. Check your heading and make a shallow turn 180 degrees to get out into the clear again.

At sea, be alert to weather conditions. Don't head out into fog. Get current weather before departure. Look for signs of weather change. Smoke clinging low is one indication that fog could be developing. If you are approaching a fog bank, turn around if you can. If you are enveloped in fog, record your position latitude and longitude right away. Steer clear of shore, remain in deep water, and, if possible, stay out of shipping channels. If you can find a safe spot of water, drop anchor, stay put with your running lights on, and wait for the fog to lift. Deploy radar deflectors if you have them.

Listen for sounds of other boats, foghorns, and waves crashing on rocks. But keep in mind that sound, both volume and direction, are distorted in fog. Look out at both the highest vantage point, and the lowest, because fog can vary in intensity.

Make noise to let others know where you are. In this situation—stuck in a fog bank and unaware of the location of other traffic—you are required to send out a sound signal every two minutes. Bang pots, blow a whistle, or sound a horn.

SNOW BLINDNESS

Although Alaska winters are known for cold and darkness, you still face a powerful amount of ultraviolet rays when the sun does rise above the horizon. The low angle of the sun and its reflections off snow, ice, and water are hazardous. Eyes can be burned from these powerful rays, even on days that appear gray. One woman reported burning her eyes on a day that was so gray that she didn't believe at first that her condition was snow blindness. You can be affected even when conditions are near twilight darkness.

If you are outdoors with no eye protection, you can use local organic materials to ward off snow blindness.

You can use ashes from a fire to blacken your cheekbones and skin under your eyes to reduce glare. Sun shields can be made out of birch bark and, if nothing else is available, a piece of cloth will serve.

You need to fashion a piece of material large enough to cover the area around your eyes from temple to temple. Mark where your pupils will be.

Cut a narrow slit horizontally about one-quarter inch on each side and about one inch long. Fasten the eye shield in place with a piece of cord. You can slice a bigger area if your vision is too restricted, but what your main concern should be is keeping the sun from doing its damage.

If you do sunburn your eyes, you will be in pain, feel as if there is grit in your eyes, experience a headache, and may be blinded temporarily. Use snow wrapped in a sock to cool the eyes. Keep them closed as much as possible.

WINTER DARKNESS & SUMMER SUN

Alaska is a perfect environment for manic depression, now known as bipolar disorder. The summer light and the winter darkness are constant in the north. In between the darkest days and those days in which there is no darkness, the change from one to the other can be rapid, up to seven minutes of loss or gain of daylight per day. Summer is a time for mania and sleepless nights when you collapse from exhaustion. Winter is a time for sleeping, having the blues when you are awake, and laughing about people in the Lower 48 states whining about Seasonal Affective Disorder.

People come up with some inventive ways to even out the extreme swings in daylight, and mood.

Seek the light. In winter, they get outside, or stare out a window in midday. The light reflected from the snowpack hits the eyeballs and helps to adjust your mood. When there is no light outside, or only shades of gray, some folks use a light box. These can be expensive, so you might want to make one yourself if your have the skills. Or, you can substitute grow lights and share a space with your plants.

Nutrition is important. According to a Fairbanks internist, you need to take extra Vitamin D during the winter because your body doesn't produce much, if any, of it during this season.

Monitor what you watch. If you watch movies or videos, choose comedies or films shot in warm, bright colors. Depressing subjects filmed in dark tones are often rejected for movie nights at home during the winter.

Maintain a regular schedule. Go to bed and get up at the same time every day, instead of letting the light dictate your schedule. If you get up with the sunrise, you will be getting up later and going to bed earlier every day. True, it is nice to brag to relatives Outside that you always get up with the dawn, but even the slowest Alaskan knows you can get up with the dawn in December and still be in bed at 10 a.m.

Exertion is a good thing. Exercise every day and outdoors if possible. All studies say the same thing about benefits of exercise. If ever there was a magic remedy, exercise is it. Exercise dispels or mitigates the lack of light, the draining cold, and the accompanying feelings of isolation and depression. If you don't have access to a gym, take a walk outdoors, cut firewood, snowshoe, ski, or shovel snow.

Moderate those cravings. Alaskans have the highest consumption of ice cream in the nation and are no slouches in the alcohol consumption department either. But to come out of the winter season looking and feeling like something other than a frat party animal, you should accept that this is a stressful time and be kind to yourself in other ways. Excessive consumption of alcohol makes depression worse and, although those sugar and fat cravings are real, giving in to them won't help in the long run.

Change your environment. If all else fails, remember you can get to Hawaii and a lot of other warm, sunny destinations in a day.

When you need darkness. In summer, use dark curtains and shades to darken your bedroom or use an eye mask while you sleep. Your body doesn't get complete rest in a lighted room. It is easy to find yourself still going at 2 a.m., so set a regular bedtime, and stick to it. If you still find it hard to sleep, set aside an hour before bedtime to settle down in a dim room. Take an eye mask on camping trips so you can sleep peacefully. Usually, you can get by with less sleep in the summer, and catch up when, all too soon, it is cold and dark again.

Author's Notes

PUBLICATIONS

Schuh, Dwight R. Modern Outdoor Survival: Outdoor gear and savvy to bring you back alive. New York: Arco 1983.

Platt, Charles. Outdoor Survival. New York: F. Watts. 1976

Merrill, Wilfred Kerner. The Survival Handbook. Winchester Press. 1972.

Alford, Monty. Wilderness Survival Guide. Portland, Ore.: Alaska Northwest Books, 1987.

Alford, Monty. Winterwise: Travel & Survival in Ice and Snow. Surrey, B.C.: Heritage House. 1999.

RCAF Survival Training School. Down But Not Out. Ottawa: Information Canada. 1973.

Alan Fry. Wilderness Survival Handbook. New York: St. Martins Press. 1981.

McManners, Hugh. The Complete Wilderness Training Book. New York: DK Pub. 1994.

Pelton, Robert Young. Come Back Alive: The Ultimate Guide to Surviving Disasters, Kidnappings, Animal Attacks, and Other Nasty Perils of Modern Travel. New York: Doubleday.1999.

Greenbank, Anthony. The Book of Survival: The Original Guide to Staying Alive in the City, the Suburbs, and the Wild Lands Beyond. New York: Hatherleigh Press. 2001, 2004.

McDougall, Len. Practical Outdoor Survival. New York: Lyons & Burford. 1992.

Johnson, Daniel A. Just in Case: A Passenger's Guide to Airplane Safety and Survival. Plenum 1984

Anderson, Eric G. Plane Safety & Survival. Aero Publishers. 1978.

Weiss, Eric A. MD. Wilderness 911: A Step by Step Guide for Medical Emergencies & Improved Care in the Back Country. Seattle: The Mountaineers; Emmaus, Pa.: Backpacker, 1998.

Fredston, Jill, Doug Felser. Snow Sense: A Guide to Evaluating Snow Avalanche Hazards. Fairbanks: Arctic Environmental Information and

Data Center, University of Alaska Fairbanks 1984. Alaska Mountain Safety Center, 1999.

Eiden, Greg, Hollomon, Kurt. Basic Training Essential Skills for Visitors, Newcomers & Native Northwesterners. Seattle: Sasquatch Books, 2001.

Piven, Joshua, Borgenicht, David. The Worst-Case Scenario Survival Handbook. San Francisco: Chronicle Books. 1999.

Angier, Bradford. How to Stay Alive in the Woods : A Complete Guide to Food, Shelter, and Self-Preservation—anywhere. New York: Black Dog & Leventhal Publishers. 2001.

VIDEOCASSETTES

Wilderness Bob's Survival Guide. No personal production credits. 50 min. Fenwick Professional Service. 1996.

Survival: Seventeen Ways to Start a Fire without a Match. Hosts: Meuninck, Jim, Mel DeWeese, Bill Forgey, Chris Clark. 60 min. Media Methods. 1997.

Stay Alive!: A Guide to Survival in Mountainous Areas. 89 min. Preston Westmoreland. Westmoreland Productions, 1993.

The 17 Most Popular Ways to Fall Out of the Sky—and How to Avoid Them., produced by Robin Sturmthal, Jack Watson. Directed by L.D. Shelby, Jack Watson. Flyright Productions. 2 hr. 25 min. 1993.

Beating the Odds: Avalanche Search and Rescue. Produced by YAK Alpine Enterprises Inc. for Canadian Avalanche Association. 48 min. 1996.

Avalanche Awareness: A Question of Balance. Produced by Sarah Conover. Alliance Communications. 30 min. 1988.

Winning the Avalanche Game. Wasatch Interpretive Association. 58 min. 1993.

Super Cubs II hardcore: Wheels and Skis. Written and produced by Jim Carkhuff. 50 min. 1997.

Carrying survival gear
in your car could save your life.

Index

D

E

F

ABOUT THE AUTHOR

Mary Ames set off for a life of adventure when she was seventeen. She hitchhiked and rode freight trains around the Lower 48. Along the way, she picked vegetables, worked as a waitress, tended bar, trapped, hunted, fished, planted trees, served as a physical therapy aide, taught children to swim, and learned to fly. All this sharpened her sense of humor. Then, she returned to college for a degree in journalism and now lives in Fairbanks, Alaska.

ABOUT THE ILLUSTRATOR

Bob Parsons is a native Alaskan, mostly confined to Anchorage, but he lived a few years in McGrath, too, scaring his mother as he played along the cutbanks of the Kuskokwim River. She ended up chaining him with the sled dogs.

Artistically he comes right out of the pages of Mad magazine. In his day, Nintendo was drawing at his cousin's table, trying to recreate the genius of Mort Drucker. "I never made it!" laments Parsons. "I always loved to draw, though, and not even a year in art school could ruin that for me. I just never quit."

Today, jazz guitar and the drawing pen seem to occupy an adversarial position in Bob's life. Hopefully someday they will become friends...

Printed in the USA
CPSIA information can be obtained
at www.ICGtesting.com
LVHW052334290923
759592LV00009B/151